THE
PLC
DASHBOARD

Implementing, Leading, & Sustaining
Your Professional Learning Community at Work®

BRIG LEANE

FOREWORD BY ROBERT EAKER

Solution Tree | Press

a division of
Solution Tree

555 North Morton Street
Bloomington, IN 47404
800.733.6786 (toll free) / 812.336.7700
FAX: 812.336.7790

email: info@SolutionTree.com
SolutionTree.com

Visit **go.SolutionTree.com/PLCbooks** to download the free reproducibles in this book.

Printed in the United States of America

FSC
www.fsc.org
FSC® C012681
The mark of
responsible forestry

Library of Congress Cataloging-in-Publication Data

Names: Leane, Brig, author.
Title: The PLC dashboard : implementing, leading, and sustaining your
   Professional Learning Community at Work / Brig Leane.
Description: Bloomington, IN : Solution Tree Press, 2025. | Includes
   bibliographical references and index.
Identifiers: LCCN 2024041386 (print) | LCCN 2024041387 (ebook) | ISBN
   9781962188715 (paperback) | ISBN 9781962188722 (ebook)
Subjects: LCSH: Professional learning communities. | Teachers--Professional
   relationships. | Educational change.
Classification: LCC LB1731 .L4235 2025 (print) | LCC LB1731 (ebook) | DDC
   371.1--dc23/eng/20241227
LC record available at https://lccn.loc.gov/2024041386
LC ebook record available at https://lccn.loc.gov/2024041387

Solution Tree
Jeffrey C. Jones, CEO
Edmund M. Ackerman, President

Solution Tree Press
President and Publisher: Douglas M. Rife
Associate Publishers: Todd Brakke and Kendra Slayton
Editorial Director: Laurel Hecker
Art Director: Rian Anderson
Copy Chief: Jessi Finn
Senior Production Editor: Suzanne Kraszewski
Proofreader: Charlotte Jones
Text and Cover Designer: Abigail Bowen
Acquisitions Editors: Carol Collins and Hilary Goff
Content Development Specialist: Amy Rubenstein
Associate Editors: Sarah Ludwig and Elijah Oates
Editorial Assistant: Anne Marie Watkins

Acknowledgments

I am thankful to stand on the shoulders of Professional Learning Communities at Work® giants—Rick and Becky DuFour, Bob Eaker, Tom Many, Mike Mattos, and Anthony Muhammad. In his last months with us, Rick said to a group of new associates that he had carried the PLC torch as far as he could, and he was passing it to all of us. To my fellow Solution Tree associates who bravely serve educators: I am honored to carry the torch with you, and I am so grateful for your friendship, insights, courage, collaboration, and counsel.

I am also thankful to collaborate with the entire team at Solution Tree; your professionalism, generosity, and kindness make me proud to further the vision to transform education worldwide to ensure learning for all. A special thank you to Claudia Wheatley for your specific guidance, feedback, friendship, encouragement, faith, and how you speak the truth in love.

To the district leaders, principals, and teachers across the country I have had the privilege of working with as a consultant: I am honored to work alongside each of you as you serve with such professionalism. Your keen insights have shaped the ideas in this book.

Thank you to Bob Eaker for your humor and wit, and especially for your willingness to write such a thoughtful foreword to this book. You have inspired me since my beginning in the PLC process.

I would also like to thank my extended family and friends who love and encourage me, and sharpen me as iron sharpens iron. To Emily, Chloe, and Kayla: Thank you for your grace in the things I've missed, and for being the best daughters a father could ask for. To my wonderful wife Kim: I could not do the work I feel called to do without your support, editing, encouragement, and love! I love life with you!

And finally, I thank Jesus for guidance and peace and seeing me through the storms of life.

Solution Tree Press would like to thank the following reviewers:

Doug Crowley
Assistant Principal
DeForest Area High School
DeForest, Wisconsin

Teresa Kinley
Humanities Teacher
Calgary, Alberta

Brad Neuendorf
Principal
Lander Valley High School
Lander, Wyoming

Bo Ryan
Principal/Solution Tree and Marzano
    Associate/Author
Ana Grace Academy of the Arts Middle School
Bloomfield, Connecticut

Christie Shealy
Director of Testing and Accountability
Anderson School District One
Williamston, South Carolina

Laurie Warner
Education Consultant
Beyond the Gray Area, LLC
Anthem, Arizona

Table of Contents

CHAPTER 3

Implementing the Seven-Step Learning Cycle **41**

CHAPTER 4

Providing Time and Support **79**

CHAPTER 5

Implementing the PLC Dashboard **107**

About the Author

Brig Leane, former principal of Fruita Middle School in Colorado, has been working in education since 2000. He has been an assistant principal and has taught at the middle and high school levels in inner-city, suburban, and rural schools. He has also been an adjunct professor at Colorado Christian University.

Under Brig's leadership as principal, Fruita's organizational health index grew from the lowest to the highest levels. This collaborative transformation propelled a school previously known for teacher independence to national Model Professional Learning Community (PLC) status, one of only three schools in the state to receive this designation. During the transformation, Fruita was the only middle school in the Mesa County Valley School District recognized for achieving student growth above the state median in every tested subject, in all grades, and with every demographic subgroup of students the state of Colorado measures. His school was recognized on Getting Smart's annual list as one of eighty-five schools in the United States educators should visit.

As a teacher, Brig learned the power of the PLC process firsthand, as his mathematics team academically grew students more than any other team, in any grade, in any tested subject in a 22,000-student school district.

Brig has presented to large and small groups of educators, and his work has been published in *Phi Delta Kappan*, *Principal Leadership*, and the Association for Supervision and Curriculum Development's online learning platform.

Education is Brig's second career, following his successful service as an officer in the U.S. Coast Guard, having attained the rank of lieutenant commander. He graduated with honors from the U.S. Coast Guard Academy with a bachelor's degree in civil engineering and served as an officer for many years on humanitarian missions around the United States. He was selected as a Troops-to-Teachers recipient and earned master's degrees in business administration and educational leadership from Colorado Mesa University.

To learn more about Brig's work, visit www.brigleane.com and follow @BrigLeane on X.

Foreword

BY ROBERT EAKER

I am frequently asked why I think the Professional Learning Communities at Work® (PLC at Work) process has not only survived but also continues to grow after more than a quarter of a century. While a number of factors account for the longevity of the process, one of the most powerful is that the practices of a high-performing PLC at Work are both practitioner driven and practitioner proven. Educators place a high value on research-based processes, practices, and materials that are practitioner developed and proven in schools and classrooms, all of which contribute to the ongoing reliance on the PLC at Work process.

Much of the power derived from practitioner-developed and proven practices and materials is that administrators and teachers find the practices not only credible, but also doable. Effective teaching and learning are complex and difficult endeavors that are often undertaken with limited time and resources. Recognizing the need to clarify and simplify the work of PLCs to make implementation more successful, Brig Leane developed the PLC Dashboard in his own school over many years. The PLC Dashboard and his seven-step plan for implementation make the PLC at Work process not only rational and logical but, equally important, doable.

Brig Leane is an accomplished school practitioner who has served in a wide variety of positions, including teacher, assistant principal, and principal; as a principal, he led his school to national Model Professional Learning Community status. Additionally, he has assisted dozens of schools and districts in effectively implementing the PLC at Work process. Along the way, Brig developed materials that serve as practical tools for those who are either getting started or working to drill deeper into the processes and practices of high-performing PLCs. This book, *The PLC Dashboard: Implementing, Leading, and Sustaining Your Professional Learning Community at Work*, is a valuable tool kit containing a plethora of practical and proven schoolwide, team, and classroom ideas, practices, and materials to strengthen your PLC implementation.

Although educators will find the entirety of this book incredibly helpful, the dashboard tool, which allows leaders to monitor the schoolwide progress and products of teams—

team by team, and task by task—has the power to transform PLC implementation. While the PLC at Work process emphasizes the need to monitor each student's learning skill by skill, Brig extends this to monitoring the work and products of each team in a meaningful, useful, and timely manner. The Dashboard is a critical tool both administrators and teachers will find useful not only in monitoring progress and products, but also in making accurate decisions about additional time and support for both students and teams, as well as extending student and team learning.

Readers will find *The PLC Dashboard* easy to read and full of materials and practices to make implementation easier; they will also find it inspirational. After reading Brig's book, one is left contemplating this challenge: For school leaders who have not started the journey of implementing the PLC at Work process, why not get started? *Here's how!* For those who are engaged in the process, why not drill deeper and get better, forever? *Here's how!* Brig continues to add to the growing body of evidence substantiating the fact that the lack of a knowledge base, the lack of "how to," is no longer a viable excuse for not implementing the PLC at Work process. Ultimately, we are left with the decision to act—to do—and *The PLC Dashboard* is a valuable guidebook to accompany you on your school improvement journey. Whether you are getting started or going deeper, it will help you keep moving forward with improved ability and greater confidence.

Introduction

When I was in the United States Coast Guard, I was involved in countless dangerous situations at sea. Once, while on patrol on a stormy night, our ship was contacted to rescue a man on a sailboat several hundred miles off the California coast. He was attempting to sail to Hawaii—alone. We later discovered, as the weather rapidly deteriorated, that the sailor in distress was blind. We had a saying in the Coast Guard: "It's not your fault, but it is your problem." Sometimes, boaters weren't prepared. Sometimes, they would forget to check the weather and end up in a storm they could have avoided. A fisherman might neglect routine maintenance, and his boat would break down at sea or even simply run out of gas. It wasn't our fault, but our lifesaving mission (our why) was clear: It was now our problem to solve.

That mindset served me well in the Coast Guard and continues to serve me well in education, where students come to school with all kinds of issues, some of which could have been prevented. Regardless, as educators, it is not our fault, but it is our challenge to ensure students learn the essential skills they need—not only for the current school year, but for life.

On that stormy night, I was one of two Coast Guardsmen who had to make the treacherous leap from our ship's small boat onto the blind man's sailboat as huge waves lifted the sailboat way above us one moment and then dropped it far below us the next. When the situation looked as good as it was going to get, we each made the leap between the two boats to rescue the man.

Likewise, in a classroom, many students are in distress and have no idea of the price they are going to pay for their poor preparation, lack of motivation, insufficient support system, or any other reasons for not succeeding in school. That's not your fault either, but it is your problem, responsibility, and even *opportunity* to solve.

Think of the storms ahead for students who do not make it successfully through the K–12 system: These great young people may struggle to meet their daily food and housing needs for themselves and their future children *for the rest of their lives*, not to mention their struggles' broader cost to society. Much is at stake, and I believe educators are among the only lifelines for so many students and their families. We are in a position to make a big difference, and the Professional Learning Communities at Work (PLC at Work) process is simply the best strategy to significantly impact both students and educators (Cottingham, Hough, & Myung, 2023; Hanson et al., 2021; Read On Arizona, 2024; Solution Tree, 2024a–c). Yet, for too many educators, important obstacles linger. Many still lack clarity on why the PLC process matters, aren't sure how to start or sustain the PLC process campuswide, or don't believe they have the time to do the work.

PLC and the Purpose of This Book

My first experience with PLC was as a high school mathematics teacher; our students had just taken an end-of-chapter common assessment on which myself and the other mathematics teacher had agreed. We discussed the number of students who missed each item on our twenty-question assessment. Some of her students missed more points on some questions, and some of mine missed more on other questions. There were many learning targets on our test, none of which we had articulated ahead of time with each other or to our students. We left our collaborative time without one change in practice, without a plan for students who had been unsuccessful—and frankly, I left thinking the PLC process (as we had carried it out) was a waste of time. As I look back now, we didn't know why we were even doing PLC work in the first place, and we certainly didn't know how.

During my master's coursework when I was an eighth-grade mathematics teacher, I read *Professional Learning Communities at Work: Best Practices for Enhancing Student Achievement* by Richard DuFour and Robert Eaker (1998). I remember thinking that what my school district called PLC did not even remotely resemble what I was reading about in the book. I also felt like I had a good reason for not working through the PLC process as designed: The other eighth-grade mathematics teacher—a former wrestling coach who had been asked to come out of retirement to take the hard-to-fill position—didn't at first appear to be someone with whom I wanted to collaborate. His name was George, and he didn't even want a computer in his classroom because he didn't like the noise of the fan. George also didn't like the smell of dry-erase markers, as he preferred chalk. Despite this, I decided to ask George if he would be willing to work with me to answer the four critical questions of a PLC (DuFour, DuFour, Eaker, Many, Mattos, & Muhammad, 2024):

1. What knowledge, skills, and dispositions should every student acquire as a result of this unit, this course, or this grade level?

2. How will we know when each student has acquired the essential knowledge and skills?

3. How will we respond when some students do not learn?

4. How will we extend the learning for those students who are already proficient? (p. 44)

To my surprise, George agreed to try it, even though no one in our building was encouraging us to use the PLC process as it was presented in the book.

I still remember George's reaction when our first common formative assessment indicated that only 14 percent of our students were proficient in our team-determined essential skills.

"But I taught it!" he yelled as he slammed his fist on the table. Even though he and I had taught it, the students hadn't learned it. While it might not have been our fault (although it also might have been our fault) that the students didn't learn what we determined to be essential, it was our problem to solve—the very thing we were hired to do.

We methodically worked through the PLC process, at least as well as I understood it. How did we do it? Our process was to determine what we wanted every student to know and be able to do, give common formative assessments, compare results, and use twenty minutes of already existing "make-up time" for reteaching interventions. George and I worked skill by skill, intervening with group after group who lacked each skill—until months later, 88 percent of the eighth-grade mathematics students had learned every skill we said was essential. It was so exciting to observe students who didn't believe in themselves learn things they didn't know they could learn! We then repeated the process with another group of essential skills.

Fast forward to the end of the school year, when George went back into retirement, and I became an assistant principal in a different school. When the state test results came out, we discovered our two-man grade 8 mathematics team had grown students more than any other teacher team, in any grade, in any tested subject in our 22,000-student school district. I became a true believer in the PLC process, and, since that time, I have experienced implementing the process at the teacher and administrative levels and now as a consultant supporting educators.

This book is for principals, instructional coaches, teacher leaders, and school district administrators who (1) have heard of and may already have some experience with the PLC at Work process, (2) want to get the process implemented right, and (3) have no time to waste. This book will help you:

- Reinforce your reasons for implementing the powerful PLC at Work process
- Learn specific implementation steps
- Identify quick wins to positively impact school culture and propel change
- Create a simple and sustainable process

My hope is to keep this book as concise as possible while providing enough guidance so that your PLC can flourish on your campus with the limited amount of time educators have available.

It is hard enough to keep a school functioning well; lack of clarity regarding the PLC process shouldn't be an added complication. Without clarity, educators will lack both the competence and confidence needed to weather the storms of true change. Too many educators haven't yet found the clarity they have needed for PLC implementation, so I am excited that this roadmap is now in your hands. I look forward to our journey through this together so that you can create a sustainable, effective process in your school. Not only will the PLC process rescue many struggling students, but it will also increase the level of hope in the outstanding educators in your school.

Creating a sustainable process is doable—and a big challenge. Regardless of where you are starting or the struggles you have encountered, let's get it right this time for the benefit of the students you serve! There are many challenges ahead, but the journey is well worth it.

Challenges for Leaders

This book is about building and sustaining a coherent process for PLC implementation while acknowledging that what is built must be manageable by teachers and school leaders who can devote only a portion of their time to the PLC process. A structure that is not manageable, is too complex, or has too many ambiguities will fail—not in one catastrophic moment, but quietly, over time, as other competing and urgent demands and challenges take priority.

When I think about principals and teacher leaders today, I have several assumptions about them.

- Many are overloaded with tasks.
- Unplanned and urgent issues come from within and outside the school.
- Staffing, including finding substitute teachers, can be challenging.
- Safety is always a concern.
- New initiatives keep coming.

Because of these and other issues; it is often challenging to start and sustain important initiatives on campus. Too often, the only energy principals and teacher leaders have left is spent just keeping school going.

Despite the challenges, the public still expects student results to improve. With good reason, the public expects accountability for the use of its dollars, and when society is spending so much on public education, it is rightfully expecting a lot in return. We have the knowledge about what we must do to improve, and students and their families are counting on us; we simply must get better results.

In addition to teachers lacking clarity about the PLC process, another reason the PLC process fails on campuses is that principals simply don't have the time or the structures to know which teams need more time and support, and even if they do know which teams need support, many are often unsure of what support to provide.

The following are a few situations I experienced working in schools that needed to improve their PLC implementation.

- A large, brand new, comprehensive high school in an affluent area that had close to 10 percent of their well-supported-at-home students failing classes
- An inner-city middle school with a first-year principal that had been scheduled to be closed within two years because of a deteriorating building and a declining neighborhood student population; teachers at the school were protesting low district pay on the street before school, during lunch, and after school
- An elementary school where 100 percent of the students were on free and reduced lunch, rated an F school by the state, with a 20 percent mobility rate
- A junior high school where a student was shot and killed between classes that could no longer get substitutes or applicants for multiple open positions because of safety fears

- A prestigious charter middle school that dropped students each semester who were not making the grade; this school examined its "proposed drop list" for an upcoming semester only to find out that every student on the list was also listed by the state as a minority
- A middle school full of independent teachers who only shared a parking lot; this school had a dozen or so staff members who considered themselves the "mean teacher group"
- A school in a district that had had three superintendents in three years; as I was working with the staff, the school was restructured because of declining enrollment

Even though these situations are diverse, many campus administrators and teacher leaders at these schools wanted to do better for the students they served, and the PLC process was successfully started or re-started on each campus.

About This Book

Many educators are at first intrigued by the idea of working together, but co-laboring to ensure student learning is hard work, and teams can struggle. In my experience with teams across the United States, educators tend to struggle with the PLC process for three main reasons.

1. They don't know why they should implement the PLC process.
2. They don't know how to implement the PLC process.
3. They don't have the time and support to implement the PLC process.

These reasons are important, because teams will struggle when they don't have the will (the why), the skill (the how), or the capacity (the time and support) to do this work. When thinking about a team that you are on or a team with which you have worked, which of these three reasons do you think caused the team to struggle? This book targets these three areas of need head-on using three main tools: (1) a seven-step learning cycle, (2) a one-page guiding template for teams and singletons, and (3) the PLC Dashboard.

Chapter 1 provides an overview of the PLC Dashboard so that readers can begin with the end in mind. This chapter introduces the focus of the book, the rationale for how chapters are sequenced, and why schools should become PLCs. Before digging into this chapter, I encourage you to think about your current answer to the question, "Why a PLC?" Chapter 1 and all subsequent chapters end with ways to tell if your school is getting PLC right (or not). In addition, chapter 1 and the rest of the book's chapters include additional resources for educators who wish to go even deeper with supporting texts.

Chapter 2 covers the importance of a teacher and administrator leadership team—a guiding coalition—and who should be on this critical team. Additionally, the chapter ensures readers share a common understanding of PLC fundamentals, the stages educators should expect as this work develops, and ideas for beginning when teachers already feel they have too much on their plates.

Chapter 3 is the most comprehensive chapter of the book, as readers learn the seven-step learning cycle (the how), with detailed information about each step. While this book is written for principals, instructional coaches, and teacher leaders, all teachers on campus will need to learn the seven-step learning cycle components to effectively carry out this work as a team or singleton.

Chapter 4 examines the time and support teams and singletons need to carry out the seven-step learning cycle expectations. A one-page template is introduced to guide teams and singletons and includes sample templates. Additional supports needed from the guiding coalition and campus administration are also explained in this chapter.

Chapter 5 builds on the previous chapters to expand on the PLC Dashboard and how this simple tool not only helps sustain the PLC process on campus over time but also rapidly illuminates when teams should celebrate and when teams need more support. Readers will learn how to build a PLC Dashboard in doable parts that allow educators to progress at their own pace from PLC initiation to sustainability.

The book concludes with an epilogue that includes some next steps and additional words of encouragement when inevitable setbacks arise, as well as an appendix that contains answers to many of the frequently asked questions about the PLC process, implementing the seven-step learning cycle, the templates to guide educators, and using the PLC Dashboard.

During the rescue involving the sailor who was blind, we could have had the mindset of, "What was he thinking, trying to make such a treacherous journey?" We might have also thought, "He put himself in this predicament; why should we go out of our way and risk our lives when he should have known better?" Amazingly, we successfully rescued the sailor, but what if he had been ungrateful to us after his rescue?

Some students will come to us with tremendous challenges, including challenges that preparation or foresight by their family could have avoided. Often, students, families, and society won't even thank us for the extra work we do to ensure all students learn the essential skills they will need now and in their future. Simply put, we must get organized to ensure every student learns what has been deemed essential because that is our job. The calling to be an educator is noble, and we willingly applied to do it; let's ensure student learning regardless of the circumstances.

Educators in schools are working extremely hard, whether they are pursuing the PLC process or not. I am proud and excited to share the lessons I have learned as I have worked alongside educators like you who daily put their hearts and souls into being educators. I want all educators to know and implement ways to get better results for the students they serve and for those educators to have even more fulfillment in the life-changing work of education.

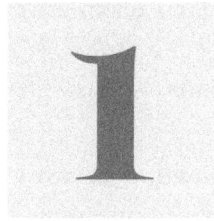

1

Beginning With the End in Mind

Knowing where you are going is the first step to getting there.

—KEN BLANCHARD

Most of us have experienced a task that seemed insurmountable. As children, we might have opened a new Lego block set to find hundreds of pieces inside that look nothing like the picture on the box. It is the precise, step-by-step instructions that lead to the assembly of a toy that looks exactly like it should. Without those instructions, assembling a Lego set to look like the picture on the box would be slow, tedious, frustrating, and nearly impossible. PLC transformation can feel the same—overwhelming and frustrating straight out of the box. As educational experts Douglas Reeves and Robert Eaker (2019) state, "There are those who begin the journey to become a professional learning community but simply do not know what to do" (p. 7). School leaders and teachers need clarity if they are going to be confident and competent in the work of PLC transformation.

Let's take a moment to consider two different principals: Principal Dakota and Principal Carolina, who are both busy leaders in their separate schools in different states. Their schools have similar demographics on similarly sized campuses, and they both have challenges and frustrations, as well as some pockets of success. Both principals have introduced the PLC process with clarity to their staff, and both made a good case for why shifting from a focus on the teaching found in traditional schools to a focus on learning in a PLC just makes sense.

Principal Dakota has a method to monitor the work of teacher teams; she knows which teams are doing well, and which ones need more time and support. Even though Principal Dakota's schedule is full, when she notices one of the teams on campus does not have an action plan to address assessment results from an essential skill, she schedules a meeting with the team that week to discuss the situation. At the beginning of staff meetings, Principal Dakota routinely takes a few screenshots from the exemplary PLC products that teams have generated to celebrate the progress at school. New and experienced teachers on Principal Dakota's campus know exactly what their teams are expected to produce, get feedback on those products, and know what will be monitored. Many of the new teachers mention how much support they feel from their teams and how glad they are to learn so much from the experienced teachers on the team.

Principal Carolina, on the other hand, does not have a plan for collecting team products; instead, she tries to join as many team meetings as possible, time permitting. Principal Carolina attempts to make sense of each team's Google Drive, but she can't tell from the folders and files how well a team is doing, or even what they are doing. When asked, Principal Carolina sadly admits to knowing that some teams are stronger than others but not knowing how effective each team really is.

Which of the two principals do you think will be able to sustain the PLC process over time? You might be wondering how you can make the reality at your school resemble the work Principal Dakota is doing. This involves three key components.

1. **The seven-step learning cycle:** A step-by-step process for collaborative teams and singletons to follow while implementing the PLC process

2. **A standardized template:** A one-page template to guide teams and singletons through the seven-step learning cycle

3. **The PLC Dashboard:** A tool for capturing the critical information from each team that allows leaders and educators from across the campus to easily assess the progress of each collaborative team and singleton as they implement the PLC process

Later, in chapters 3, 4, and 5, we will explore the PLC process (as detailed in the seven-step learning cycle), the template, and the PLC Dashboard in detail. This chapter provides a brief overview of why implementing the PLC process is imperative for schools and districts along with an overview of the PLC Dashboard tool.

Why PLC?

While some teachers might say to leaders, "Just tell me what you want me to do," it is best not to teach PLC practices without also helping teachers gain a common understanding of why schools should become PLCs. PLC experts Richard DuFour, Rebecca DuFour, Robert Eaker, Thomas W. Many, Mike Mattos, and Anthony Muhammad (2024) reinforce this by reminding us that "one of the most common mistakes school administrators make in the implementation of improvement initiatives is to focus exclusively on *how* while being inattentive to *why*" (p. 6). Too many administrators make this common mistake.

Suppose someone were to ask you, "Why are we doing this PLC work?"—what would you say? Take a few moments to think about how you would answer that question; many leaders of would-be PLCs do not have an adequate response that justifies the increased workload for educators who are a part of an effective PLC. While there are challenges in implementing the PLC process, there are many reasons why a learning-focused, collaborative culture sustained over time makes sense. Some of the reasons for educators to fully embrace the PLC process include the following.

- It is backed by research.
- It facilitates job-embedded professional learning.
- It creates authentic connectedness to others.
- It represents equity in action.
- It supports new teachers.
- It allows experienced teachers to share their vast knowledge.
- It is respectful of teachers.
- It combats poverty and increases hope.

Let's look at each one of these reasons to ensure we have a shared understanding of why the shift from teaching to learning in a PLC at Work matters.

Backed by Research

If someone were to ask you, "What is the number one factor for improving student learning?" what would you say? Would it be having a certified teacher? Ensuring every student has a computer? Teachers developing positive relationships with students? Each of these reasons has an impact, but they are not the *number one factor*.

According to educational researcher Robert Marzano (2003; Eaker & Marzano, 2020), creating a guaranteed and viable curriculum is the number one factor for increased levels of student learning. One of the main tasks of educators in a PLC is to determine the guaranteed and viable curriculum—the essential skills that every student will learn, regardless of the teacher to whom they are assigned (guaranteed), within the amount of time available for students to learn those skills, even when some students need more time and support to do so (viable).

Likewise, according to educational researcher John Hattie (2009, 2023), whose meta-analysis encompasses tens of millions of students to determine what has the most visible impact on learning, some of the highest impacts to student achievement happen when:

- Teachers have clarity of the expected learnings and communicate success criteria to their students.
- Feedback occurs from teachers to students about the task they completed and from students to teachers about what they know, where they made errors, and where they have misconceptions.

Hattie (2023) also concludes that educators should:

- Work together to evaluate their impact
- Have high expectations for all students
- Be transparent in converting these high expectations through success criteria
- Teach students to take on the challenge to aim high
- Create fair and high-trust classrooms in which errors and mistakes are seen as opportunities to learn
- Continually seek feedback about their impact
- Have a relentless focus on learning

Each of these actions Marzano and Hattie identify is an integral part of the PLC process. A relentless focus on learning combined with clarity of the expected learnings is what teachers achieve in a PLC when working together to determine what they want students to know and be able to do (DuFour et al., 2024). Working together in a PLC to evaluate their impact allows educators to determine how they will know if students have learned, what they will do when students have not learned, and what they will do when students have learned (DuFour et al., 2024). Educators seeking feedback could be summed up as "professionals who are learning in community" or PLCs, working for the benefit of the students they serve.

The PLC process requires that teachers intervene to support students who are struggling (DuFour et al., 2024). Intervention experts Mike Mattos, Austin Buffum, Janet Malone, Luis F. Cruz, Nicole Dimich, and Sarah Schuhl (2025) state that when a response to intervention (RTI) or multitiered system of support (MTSS) system is in place, with timely, targeted, and systematic interventions for all students who need them, student learning increases. To realize increased student learning, a successful intervention system is critical; however, an effective RTI or MTSS system isn't possible until a school first develops high-functioning collaborative teams. The PLC process, with its focus on collaborative teaming, sets the groundwork for a well-functioning RTI system.

Hattie's (2023) research indicates that collective teacher efficacy has a larger effect on student learning than any other variable. This highly impactful state can occur when teacher teams who have worked through the PLC process many times over multiple years become so confident that all students assigned to their team will learn the essentials it becomes a self-fulfilling prophecy. When collaborative teams of teachers have had the PLC process in place over several years, having learned together in each unit what works best for students (including students with dyslexia or other learning disabilities, lack of knowledge of English, or lack of support from home), the team can approach collective teacher efficacy.

Includes Job-Embedded Professional Learning

Think back to some professional development you experienced in the past. Was it engaging? Was it helpful to the students you serve? Was it a "one and done" professional development that wasn't revisited or reinforced? To be effective, professional development should be job-embedded and ongoing (Croft, Coggshall, Dolan, Powers, & Killion, 2010).

Consider three teachers who have just given a common formative assessment in class asking students to make a logical inference from a text. They are now ready to share their results with the intent of finding out what teaching strategies are working best in the challenging task of having students make a logical inference. The first teacher on the team has 27 percent of students proficient, the second has 33 percent proficiency, and the third has 74 percent proficiency. What everyone on the team should want to know is, What did the third teacher do to achieve a higher level of proficiency? This job-embedded collaboration continues in the next unit, where the second teacher gets 100 percent of her English language learners to proficiency, while the other teachers are well below 50 percent proficient. Asking the same question—What did that teacher do?—shows the ongoing nature of professional development within the PLC process.

When this cycle of collective inquiry happens repeatedly after each common formative assessment on essential learning targets the team has agreed all students must learn, the learning for the teachers is job-embedded and ongoing—the epitome of effective professional development!

Promotes Authentic Connectedness to Others

If you have ever been a part of a team—a club, sports team, or music or volunteer group—you have most likely developed a unique bond with your teammates. In team situations, individuals work together to overcome challenges, which frequently involve sacrifice on everyone's part. Those who stick with the team and contribute share the joy of their successes and the sadness of their shortcomings.

International bestselling author Sebastian Junger (2016) states in *Tribe: On Homecoming and Belonging* that humans have a basic need to feel connected to others. Even when the work is hard, the satisfaction of working together on a worthwhile goal is mutually encouraging, creates stronger bonds, and can be fun. There is simply something special about being connected in meaningful work with others that does not exist when working in isolation.

This same synergy occurs in a PLC when teachers determine together what all students must learn in a unit of study, give a common formative assessment to determine if the students have learned it, and then work together on the challenge of intervening and extending the learning from the results of that assessment for all students.

Represents Equity in Action

In *Leading PLCs at Work Districtwide*, authors Robert Eaker, Mike Hagadone, Janel Keating, and Meagan Rhoades (2021) state, "The greatest equity issue in American public education is the lack of a guaranteed and viable curriculum" (p. 94). In a guaranteed and viable curriculum, all students, regardless of the teacher to whom they are assigned, have access to the same curriculum and have the same opportunity to learn. A guaranteed and viable curriculum removes the practice of "educational lottery," where some students have the benefit of learning the essential knowledge and skills and others do not have access to the same curriculum because of the teacher they have. In PLCs, collaborative teams of teachers ensure all students learn the same essential skills. In addition, the subsequent response when students don't learn is not up to the individual teacher but rather to the team of teachers who are part of a larger system that has been set up to ensure well-planned interventions take place. If students continue to struggle, these teams create additional attempts to ensure proficiency for each student who encounters difficulty. This is equity in action. As *Ruthless Equity* author Ken Williams (2022) states:

> The questions of *can they learn*? or *can't they learn*? are no longer relevant.
> This leaves us with only one question that matters. The only question the
> pursuit of equity answers: How will we get every student there? (p. 55)

The real work of teams in a PLC is simply that: ensuring every student learns everything the team or singleton determines to be essential.

Provides New Teacher Support

There is a significant and disturbing trend in education regarding new teachers: Fewer teachers are entering the profession, and many teachers new to the profession are not staying (Aldeman, 2022). In a profession with low pay, waning respect, increased public scrutiny, and high public accountability for academic results, it is no wonder many teachers are leaving.

Despite these challenges, there are new teachers in schools, and there are things we can do to make them feel like their job is doable. Imagine a teacher who is new to the profession who is given only keys to their classroom, a copy of the state standards, and a curriculum. This is not enough. New teachers struggle with many issues, including classroom management, lack of resources, and feeling overwhelmed. These and other challenges can seem insurmountable. However, when those same teachers are on a meaningful collaborative team, they thrive because they get the support they need because the team determines essential learning targets, teaches each unit, and works together on interventions when students don't learn.

Captures the Knowledge of Experienced Teachers

What happens to the knowledge of an experienced teacher when they leave the school building, whether they are retiring or moving into other positions? In traditional schools, their knowledge and skills working with students and parents leave the school with them. However, if they have been members of meaningful collaborative teams, their knowledge has been dispersed to support the learning and development of their teammates—a powerful legacy for those who have served students with such professionalism for so long. Many experienced teachers are eager to share what they know. By effectively engaging in the PLC process, structures are intentionally in place to capture some of the knowledge that these great educators will otherwise take with them when they leave.

Is Respectful of Teachers

When a school or a district decides to implement the PLC process, they are saying by their actions that they believe if they give teachers the structures, time, and support, those teachers will be able to implement PLC practices, such as answering the four critical questions of a PLC within a collaborative team. While the PLC process has some "tight" or non-negotiable components, it also has many areas that are "loose," where teachers have the flexibility to personalize implementation. For instance, while some curricula are scripted, the PLC process encourages teaching that is, as Robert Marzano (2019) says, both an art and a science. Teachers should be allowed to teach in ways that best fit their style, so long as they don't lose sight of the fact that those practices must be getting positive results. Teachers who have an interest in trying something new, such as a flipped classroom or a more student-centered learning environment, should be encouraged to try out their new instructional methods, even if the other teachers on the team don't choose to teach the same way. It is respectful to allow teachers to teach the essential skills in their own way, and it is also reasonable to then expect them to compare their results with their colleagues who may or may not have taught in a similar way.

Combats Poverty and Provides Hope

Educators can usually think of a few students who have given up on themselves. Often these students have lost motivation, perhaps because they have experienced repeated failure. Sometimes, these students come from families in chaos, or perhaps they have too few people influencing them to do well in school. These students are in distress, and if a course change is not made, many will become adults who struggle to even meet their basic needs. Educators are in a perfect position to make a big difference for these students. When learning is broken up into smaller, manageable chunks of essential skills, and when the importance of those chunks are made clear to students and followed up with quick feedback and targeted intervention, many of those students who might otherwise give up on themselves will learn they are capable, and motivation can increase (DuFour et al., 2024; Hattie, 2023). This is because nothing increases hope in a student like accomplishing something they thought was challenging. Accomplishment builds on accomplishment, and eventually, students who might otherwise drop out of school into a life of poverty may stay in school long enough to access opportunities only open to the educated. It is a joy for educators to see struggling learners succeed, and more joy makes for a better working environment, which helps reduce turnover.

These are just some of the reasons that establish the rationale for becoming a PLC where student learning is the priority. There are excellent resources that provide in-depth information about the foundational aspects of PLC at Work, such as *Learning by Doing: A Handbook for Professional Learning Communities at Work, Fourth Edition* (DuFour et al., 2024), *School Improvement for All: A How-To Guide for Doing the Right Work* (Kramer & Schuhl, 2017), and *Taking Action: A Handbook for RTI at Work™, Second Edition* (Mattos et al., 2025). I advise you to seek out these resources for a comprehensive look at the PLC process and the many reasons for implementation.

PAUSE AND REFLECT

Which of the reasons listed here would you add to your answer to the question at the start of this chapter if someone asked you, "Why a PLC?"

A Focus on Learning

When working in schools to help educators understand the why of PLC, I find it beneficial to work with them to ensure an understanding of the first big idea of a PLC: a focus on learning (DuFour et al., 2024). I begin by having teachers read an excerpt on a focus on learning from *Learning by Doing* (DuFour et al., 2024; see figure 1.1, page 14). After teachers read about a focus on learning, I ask them to state their reasons for why the PLC process makes sense to implement on their campus. Teachers could do this work individually at first, and then share their reasons with a colleague, and then that pair shares with a larger group. School leaders (or the leadership team or guiding coalition) responsible for leading implementation then share their list of why a PLC. Teachers then share which of the reasons on the leaders' list resonate the most with them, continuing the discussion of whys again with those around them, followed by sharing a few reasons out loud to the larger group. This helps everyone see different perspectives on why the work ahead is being done and can significantly and positively impact the change process. Figure 1.1 (page 14) is a guide you and your guiding coalition can use to facilitate this activity. Leaders will need the following materials for

"Why a PLC?" Activity Guide

A Focus on Learning (From *Learning by Doing: A Handbook for Professional Learning Communities at Work* (DuFour et al., 2024)

The first (and the biggest) of the big ideas is based on the premise that the fundamental purpose of the school is to ensure that all students learn at high levels (grade level or higher). This focus on and commitment to the learning of each student is the very essence of a learning community.

When a school or district functions as a PLC, educators within the organization embrace high levels of learning for all students as both the reason the organization exists and the fundamental responsibility of those who work within it. To achieve this purpose, the members of a PLC create and are guided by a clear and compelling vision of what the organization must become to help all students learn. They make collective commitments, clarifying what each member will do to create such an organization, and they use results-oriented goals to mark their progress. Members work together to clarify exactly what each student must learn, monitor each student's learning on a timely basis, provide systematic interventions that ensure students receive additional time and support for learning when they struggle, and extend learning when students have already mastered the intended outcomes.

A corollary assumption is that if the organization is to become more effective in helping all students learn, the adults in the organization must also be continually learning. Therefore, structures are created to ensure staff members engage in job-embedded learning as part of their routine work practices.

There is no ambiguity or hedging regarding this commitment to learning. Whereas many schools operate as if their primary purpose is to ensure students are taught or are merely provided with an opportunity to learn, PLCs are dedicated to the idea that their organizations exist to ensure all students actually acquire the essential knowledge, skills, and dispositions of each unit, course, and grade level. Every potential organizational practice, policy, and procedure is assessed based on this question: "Will this ensure higher levels of learning for our students?" All the other characteristics of a PLC flow directly from this epic shift in assumptions about the purpose of the school. (p. 18)

Materials, Activity Steps, and Discussion Questions

Materials needed: Notecards or sticky notes, the reproducible for the "A Focus on Learning" excerpt from Learning by Doing (DuFour et al., 2024; visit **go.SolutionTree.com/PLCbooks** to download a free reproducible), and pens.

1. Ask teachers to read the excerpt from *Learning by Doing* individually, highlighting sentences or phrases that stand out to them and noting why.

2. Ask teachers to pair and share what stood out to them and why with a partner.

3. Have teachers answer the following question individually at first on a notecard or a sticky note: "If someone were to ask you why a school would want to become a professional learning community, what would you say?"

4. Have teachers stand and meet with a partner to share what they wrote on their cards.

5. As a whole group, ask teachers to share one of the reasons they shared with their partner.

6. Have the guiding coalition (or you, as the leader) share more reasons from this chapter for why a PLC that apply to your school.

7. Ask teachers to share back at their seats in small groups of three or four teachers which of the reasons shared by the guiding coalition also matter to them.

FIGURE 1.1: "Why a PLC?" activity guide.

*Visit **go.SolutionTree.com/PLCbooks** to download a free reproducible version of this figure.*

this activity: notecards or sticky notes, the reproducible for the "A Focus on Learning" excerpt from *Learning by Doing* (DuFour et al., 2024) from figure 1.1 (visit **go.SolutionTree.com /PLCbooks** for a free reproducible), and pens.

In addition to the "Why a PLC?" activity, leaders and the guiding coalition should ask teachers to share often about the impact the PLC process is having on students who struggle at first with learning essential knowledge and skills and about the impact the process is having on educators in the building.

According to the Harvard Business Review (2023) *HBR Guide to Executing Your Strategy*, it is reasonable that some educators will mourn what will be lost on the PLC journey, and the internal acceptance of this process may take some time. Educators who were taught the same way they now teach may grieve or even resist making some of the shifts the PLC process requires. It may be devastating for some who feel confident in how they teach to suddenly feel less competent. Teachers may feel threatened to share the results of how students performed with their colleagues for fear of being judged as less than effective. Teachers may also feel a sense of loss in the autonomy they have had to teach whatever they wanted, without input from the collaborative team. Due to these and many other feelings of loss teachers may experience, I recommend giving teachers a chance to share their feelings of loss in a small group.

In addition to listing the losses, it might also be helpful for them to be able to express what they don't know and what they will need to learn. Leaders on campuses who seek to understand how experienced educators feel about the transition to becoming a PLC can be enlightened and guided in determining the additional training and resources the staff may need.

Key Information for Leaders

The main purpose of school is not to simply teach the curriculum or cover the content but to ensure students acquire important knowledge and skills, along with habits of success, and have the ability to apply their learning to new situations and problems they will encounter in the future (Horn, 2021; Wiggins & McTighe, 2008). To fulfill this purpose, educational leaders must be able to see that learning is progressing. They don't have time to waste; they need specific, clear information on which teams are doing well and which teams need more time and support. If they cannot get this critical information quickly, they won't know to provide it and will most likely turn their attention to other urgent matters and inadvertently lose their focus on learning.

To know whether student learning is progressing, a principal might try several strategies. A principal might attempt to attend every team meeting to provide guidance and to ensure teams are focused on the right work. However, this is unsustainable from a time standpoint, and it is also too leader-centered. Other leaders expect to see agendas from teacher teams as their method to monitor team progress, or they try collecting minutes from collaborative team meetings. While having a team agenda is a key to an effective meeting, working through an agenda does not necessarily mean teams stay focused on the four PLC critical questions during their collaborative team time. For some teachers, producing these items feels like busy work. For administrators, reviewing agendas and meeting minutes is an ineffective use of time; any team could produce those items, even ineffective teams. Other leaders attempt to locate team products within an often-overwhelming Google Drive or similar shared archive.

In one school I supported, I asked the principal how teams were doing with the PLC process. He replied, "They are doing well." I asked him how he knew. He said he looked in team Google Drives. I asked him for access to those drives. The kindergarten team had forty-two folders with all types of PLC labels, such as "common formative assessments" and "team essentials." The grade 1 team had twenty-five folders with similar names. Within each folder, there were all sorts of different documents. The other teams were all over the place as well. I told the principal what I had seen and asked how he *really* knew how teams were doing. "I have my hunches," he replied with a smile.

Rather than spending time on these ineffective attempts at monitoring, leaders should have a process for reviewing actual team products, such as common formative assessments, team plans for intervention and extension, and student results. PLC experts Mike Mattos, Richard DuFour, Rebecca DuFour, Robert Eaker, and Thomas W. Many (2016) note that reviewing these products is important "to see if teams understand the work to be done, if they are getting it done, and the quality with which they are getting it done" (p. 61). They explain that this puts leaders in the position to support struggling teams and provides better insight into the work of a team. They ask, what is better—"having minutes that say the team wrote a common formative assessment or actually looking at the common assessment" (Mattos et al., 2016, p. 61)? The PLC Dashboard is the ideal solution designed to help educators organize and track the specific products Mattos and colleagues mention.

The PLC Dashboard Overview

Schools that want the PLC process to flourish must get organized to ensure every student learns every learning target collaborative teams and singletons have identified as essential. When I began to track team products as an administrator, I started with a simple pencil-and-paper checklist for each team and their products. Teams printed out their products, turned them in to me, and I tabulated how teams were progressing. I communicated team status to the guiding coalition and provided support to teams that needed it. As I began working with school leaders across the United States, it became apparent that those leaders needed to know how their teams were progressing as well. I started with a four-page template to guide teams and helped leaders build a system to tabulate on bulletin boards or Google Sheets which teams had completed the template. The template and the tabulation methods got lots of feedback and were refined for simplicity and clarity; they are now consolidated in a streamlined customizable spreadsheet I call the PLC Dashboard.

The PLC Dashboard is a visual snapshot for educators to use to:

- Quickly monitor progress across the school
- Collect and organize teams' and singleton's expected product, capturing both student and teacher learning
- Help a guiding coalition guide the PLC process
- Directly access links to the actual products themselves

- Determine which teams and singletons need more support
- Find aspects of the PLC process to celebrate

These PLC-related products generated by each team and singleton include Essential Learning Target Plans, the annual list of essential learning targets, team norms, the common formative assessments teams are using, and student results spreadsheets. With the PLC Dashboard, all educators on campus can observe each other's progress and have access to samples of other teams' products to help improve everyone's work within the PLC.

Consider the following example from an elementary school using the PLC Dashboard. Let's say it is February and the PLC Dashboard columns in figure 1.2 are available for all school leaders and educators to view. These columns in the spreadsheet show each collaborative team and singleton and the number of Essential Learning Target Plans each team has so far completed, with the target being at least eight plans for the year. The Essential Learning Target Plan template is a one-page, succinct summary of a team's work through the four critical questions of a PLC. It captures student and teacher learning of standards that teams and singletons have unpacked into essential learning targets. This tool is explored in detail in chapter 5 (page 107).

If the goal for the school year for this school is for teams and singletons to complete a minimum of eight Essential Learning Target Plans, which team appears to need more time and support? If you answered grade 2, you are correct. Grade 2 has only two Essential Learning Target Plans completed, and this is a problem in February, with more than half of the school year completed. This simple visual allows school leaders and educators to quickly ascertain which teams and singletons are on pace to meet the goal and which teams need more support. Importantly, the PLC Dashboard visually alerts the grade 2 team that they are behind with their Essential Learning Target Plan expectations and must push themselves to catch up. In addition to the information in the

A	B
Teams and Singletons	**Number of Completed Essential Learning Target Plans**
Kindergarten	5
Grade 1	6
Grade 2	2
PE	5
Music	7

FIGURE 1.2: A Simplified PLC Dashboard

Dashboard page in figure 1.2 that reveals which teams need more assistance, the tool also highlights teams to be acknowledged and celebrated. The music singleton, for example, is close to the goal of eight plans completed; this should be acknowledged.

The PLC Dashboard examples you will see in this chapter are not what your Dashboard will look like at the start. Yours will be much simpler in the beginning, and it will build over years to be like the ones shown in the rest of this chapter. I am showing these to you so that you have a picture of what your dashboard may become.

You can obtain access to the PLC Dashboard template by visiting **www.BrigLeane.com /PLCDashboard**. I built the template in Google Sheets, which is an ideal platform to host your PLC Dashboard as it allows easy access, and entries in each field can be hyperlinked. Chapter 5 (page 107) will guide you from your initiating dashboard to dashboards that will eventually look like the ones that follow here.

Figures 1.3 and 1.4 (page 20) show a dashboard example and explain some of the parts. This introduction provides a picture and a brief explanation.

Column A in figure 1.3 is a partial listing of teams and singletons on campus (abbreviated for the purposes of this book). Column B shows the specific Essential Learning Target Plans (ELTPs) teams and singletons have completed. Column C shows which Essential Learning Target Plan SMART goals the teams have met or exceeded. Column E captures the next steps teams and singletons are planning to take or have taken to improve any shortfalls indicated in columns B and C. School administrators take responsibility for ensuring teams and singletons keep all columns up to date. On the spreadsheet, in column D, colors indicate when tasks are on time and late. Red (darker shading in figure 1.3) shows when it has been more than a month since the column has been updated, and green (lighter shading) is for columns that have been updated within the month. For example, the principal turns all of the greens to red at the end of each month.

While figure 1.3 shows the big picture, figure 1.4 (page 20) has links to the specific PLC products. Figure 1.4 shows an example of the team and singleton information tab. Column A is once again a listing of all teams and singletons on campus. Column B lists their common planning period for teams to meet. Column C hyperlinks to the team's norms. Column D links to each team's yearly list of essential learning targets. Column E links to the team calendars. Columns F through I have subcolumns that link to the Essential Learning Target Plan for each learning target and then provide a place for teams to record the percentage of students proficient across all classes. Administrators are responsible for setting up this tracking page, while collaborative teams and singletons are responsible for updating the percent currently proficient column for each essential learning target. Teams and singletons are also responsible for updating and linking to the norms, the yearly list of essential learning targets (when completed), the team calendar, and each Essential Learning Target Plan. Remember that the figures in this chapter introduce you to what your PLC Dashboard will *eventually* look like; the dashboard is developed over time, as explained in detail in chapter 5 (page 107).

When educators understand the reasons for becoming a PLC covered in this chapter, using the PLC Dashboard as a tool to know if learning is taking place just makes sense. However, to understand the complete value of the PLC Dashboard and the thinking behind it, educators will need to have clarity on the collaborative work they do in the PLC process. The seven-step learning cycle covered in chapter 3 (page 41) connects the work teams do in a PLC to the dashboard tool. However, before schools dive into how the PLC process is detailed in the seven-step learning cycle, school leadership must prepare, which is the focus of the next chapter.

NEXT STEPS

Based on what you've learned in this chapter, what two or three next steps will you take to ensure staff know why the school should operate as a PLC?

Teams	Completed Essential Learning Target Plans	SMART Goals Achieved	Date	Next Steps to Improve Columns B and C on this Spreadsheet
ELA Teams				
Grade 7 ELA	1, 2, 3	1, 2, 3	1/8/25	Complete essential data and planner for 4 during meeting on 1/23/25.
Grade 8 ELA	1, 2, 3, 4	1, 3, 4	1/9/25	Meet one on one with students from essential learning target 2 who are still not proficient even with Tier 2 intervention.
Grade 9 ELA	1, 2, 3, 4	1, 2, 3, 4, 5	2/5/25	Go back and complete ELTP 5.
Mathematics Teams				
Grade 7 Mathematics	1, 2, 3, 4	1	2/7/25	Reinforce combining like terms on essential learning target 2 and give version 3 of common formative assessments (CFAs) to improve column C.
Grade 8 Mathematics	1, 2, 3	1	2/9/25	Provide more Tier 2 interventions for ELTs 2 and 3 on 2/20/24.
Grade 9 Mathematics	1, 2, 3, 4	1, 2, 3, 4	2/9/25	We are finishing up grading CFA 5 and entering data to spreadsheet.
Science Teams				
Grade 7 Science	1, 2, 3, 4, 5	1, 2, 3, 4	2/2/25	Students not proficient on essential learning target 4 will be pulled out during Seminar for more support.
Grade 8 Science	1, 2, 3, 4	1, 2, 3	2/8/25	Complete the last two prompts on ELTP 5.
Grade 9 Science	1, 2, 3, 4, 5	1, 2, 3, 4, 5	2/5/25	We will continue to use Tier 2 intervention for essential learning target 1.
Social Studies Teams				
Grade 7 Social Studies	1, 2, 3, 4	1, 3, 4	2/2/25	Use Tier 2 activities (note stems) for essential learning target 2.
Grade 8 Social Studies	1, 3, 4, 5	1, 2, 3, 4, 5	2/2/25	We will complete essential learning target 2 on 2/18/24.
Grade 9 Social Studies	1, 2, 3, 4, 5, 6	1, 2, 3, 4, 5, 6	2/2/25	Incorporate more activities such as Quiz, Quiz, Trade when reteaching.
CTE Singletons				
Career Development	1, 2, 3, 4	3	2/2/25	Continue intervening on ELTP 1 in class
Computer Science	1, 2, 4, 5	1, 2, 3, 4, 5	1/23/25	Complete ELTP 3 on 2/13/24.
FACS	1, 2, 3	1, 2	1/23/25	Complete ELTP 4.

*ELTP = Essential Learning Target Plan; ELT = essential learning target; ▇ = not updated, and ▨ = updated.

Source: Adapted from Hot Springs Junior Academy, Hot Springs, Arkansas, 2024. Used with permission.

FIGURE 1.3: PLC Dashboard sample.

	A	B	C	D	E	F		G		H		I	
						Essential Learning Target 1		**Essential Learning Target 2**		**Essential Learning Target 3**		**Essential Learning Target 4**	
	Teams and Singletons	**Team Planning Time**	**Norms**	**Yearly list of Essential Learning Targets**	**Team Calendar**	ELTP	Percent Currently Proficient	ELTP	Percent Currently Proficient	ELTP	Percent Currently Proficient	ELTP	Percent Currently Proficient
ELA Teams													
	Grade 7 ELA	Block 3	Norms	List	Dates	ELTP1	80%	ELTP 2	77%	ELTP 3	61%	ELTP 4	50%
	Grade 8 ELA		Norms	List	Dates	ELTP1	80%	ELTP 2	81%	ELTP 3	79%	ELTP 4	65%
	Grade 9 ELA		Norms	List	Dates	ELTP1	84%	ELTP 2	76%	ELTP 3	66%	ELTP 4	71%
Mathematics Teams													
	Grade 7 Mathematics	Block 4	Norms	List	Dates	ELTP1	55%	ELTP 2	61%	ELTP 3	30%	ELTP 4	18%
	Grade 8 Mathematics		Norms	List	Dates	ELTP1	81%	ELTP 2	91%	ELTP 3	67%	ELTP 4	
	Grade 9 Mathematics		Norms	List	Dates	ELTP1	85%	ELTP 2	76%	ELTP 3	86%	ELTP 4	86%
Science Teams													
	Grade 7 Science	Block 1	Norms	List	Dates	ELTP1	68%	ELTP 2	81%	ELTP 3	81%	ELTP 4	84%
	Grade 8 Science		Norms	List	Dates	ELTP1	66%	ELTP 2	71%	ELTP 3	70%	ELTP 4	
	Grade 9 Science		Norms	List	Dates	ELTP1	82%	ELTP 2	81%	ELTP 3	90%	ELTP 4	75%
Social Studies Teams													
	Grade 7 Social Studies	Block 2	Norms	List	Dates	ELTP1	71%	ELTP 2	68%	ELTP 3	74%	ELTP 4	89%
	Grade 8 Social Studies		Norms	List	Dates	ELTP1	76%	ELTP 2	72%	ELTP 3	76%	ELTP 4	84%
	Grade 9 Social Studies		Norms	List	Dates	ELTP1	90%	ELTP 2	88%	ELTP 3	80%	ELTP 4	91%
CTE Singletons													
	Career Development	Block 2	Norms	List	Dates	ELTP1	77%	ELTP 2	80%	ELTP 3	75%	ELTP 4	95%
	Computer Science	Block 4	Norms			ELTP1	66%	ELTP 2	64%	ELTP 3	55%	ELTP 4	
	FACS	Block 2	Norms			ELTP1	68%	ELTP 2	24%	ELTP 3	31%	ELTP 4	

*ELTP = Essential Learning Target Plan

Source: Hot Springs Junior Academy, 2023, Hot Springs, Arkansas. Used with permission.

FIGURE 1.4: Team and singleton information tab example from the PLC Dashboard.

Summary

School leaders simply must have a way to rapidly determine how teams and singletons are progressing at ensuring student learning of the essential learning targets. The PLC Dashboard does this, and yet without educators across campus having clarity on why they are doing all this work in the first place, the work can seem like just one more thing to do. If educators don't share a common understanding of why, they will lose their way, but when they get organized behind a common reason for what they are doing, change can happen.

Take a moment to pause and reflect on your current situation after reading this chapter. What evidence do you have that you are getting PLC implementation right, and what evidence do you have that you aren't there yet? After reflecting, explore the suggested resources for further study individually or with your teams.

PAUSE AND REFLECT

Evidence you are getting it right:

- You have more confidence for how to start and sustain the PLC process on campus.
- Teachers can share their perspectives on why their school might want to implement the PLC process.
- School leaders desire to develop a method to know which teams need more time and support to work most effectively as collaborative teams and singletons.
- We as a school want to move from "PLC lite" to deep PLC implementation.

Evidence you aren't there yet:

- Administration wants to jump right in to using the PLC Dashboard without engaging teachers in the reasons why to start and sustain the PLC work.
- Administration wants to use the PLC Dashboard as an accountability method to embarrass some and reward other teachers and teams.

What is a strength you are already doing that you could acknowledge and celebrate?

RESOURCES FOR FURTHER STUDY

- Chapter 1 in *Learning by Doing: A Handbook for Professional Learning Communities at Work* (Fourth Edition) by Richard DuFour, Rebecca DuFour, Robert Eaker, Thomas W. Many, Mike Mattos, and Anthony Muhammad (2024)

- The Introduction in *How to Leverage PLCs for School Improvement* by Sharon V. Kramer (2015)

- The Introduction in *Starting a Movement: Building Culture From the Inside Out in Professional Learning Communities* by Kenneth C. Williams and Tom Hierck (2015)

2

Getting Ready

It is time for our profession to become wise. It is time to stop waiting for others. It is time for every educator to take personal responsibility for helping bring the PLC process to life in his or her school or district.

—RICHARD DUFOUR, REBECCA DUFOUR, ROBERT EAKER,
THOMAS W. MANY, AND MIKE MATTOS

After exploring the why of PLC with staff, school leaders should then clarify how the PLC process will be implemented. If implementation is not well planned, schools can experience false starts that lead to frustration. A properly planned and executed rollout of the PLC process minimizes many of the potential challenges, allowing momentum to build along with development of a robust PLC Dashboard.

This chapter covers the getting ready phase of PLC implementation, so let's get ready, go!, and then get set! No, you didn't read that wrong. Education experts consider getting ready, going, and then getting set to be the most effective strategy when an organization is undergoing major reform (DuFour & Fullan, 2013; Fullan, 1993; Marzano, Waters, & McNulty, 2005). According to these experts, in the beginning, it is important for teachers to learn about the work to be done, then start that work with a bias for action, and then eventually set the foundational elements of a PLC at Work (the pillars—mission, vision, collective commitments, and goals; DuFour et al., 2024). This way, teachers can have some experience with the PLC process so they know what they are committing to when the school later creates their shared foundational pillars.

Get ready is the learn-together stage. This stage involves the preparation steps for both administrators and guiding coalitions. This chapter covers the get-ready stage. *Go* is the learn-by-doing stage. Teachers at this stage have enough information to begin working through the seven-step learning cycle in chapter 3 (page 41). *Get set* begins after teams and singletons have made their first attempts at taking essential learning targets through the seven-step learning cycle. This could be several months after the go stage has begun. The guiding coalition should at that time begin to build consensus on a concise mission focused on the fundamental purpose of learning at grade level or higher for all students. This mission work is addressed more fully in chapter 4 (page 79) as it does not necessarily need to be completed yet.

The main preparatory actions for administrators (and guiding coalitions, once established) in the get-ready phase are as follows.

1. Establish a guiding coalition.

2. Learn and communicate PLC fundamentals.

3. Determine collaborative teams and singletons.

4. Explain the stages of team development.

5. Reiterate team and singleton expectations.

6. Monitor the work of collaborative teams and singletons.

Establish a Guiding Coalition

There is a saying, "If you want to go fast, go alone; if you want to go far, go together." In the ongoing PLC process, you want to go far, so the work must be done together, and that requires strong and broad leadership. No leader has all the knowledge and skills to provide all professional development, answer all questions, and meet the innumerable needs of a staff making the transition from a focus on teaching to a focus on learning in a PLC. Administrators have a critical role in the success of the PLC process on campus that includes many different tasks; an important task early on is to create and sustain a guiding coalition. Mattos and colleagues (2016) define a *guiding coalition* as follows:

> A guiding coalition is an alliance of key members of an organization who are specifically charged with leading a change process through predictable turmoil. Members of the coalition should include opinion leaders—people who are so respected within the organization that others are likely to follow their lead. Members of the guiding coalition should have shared objectives and high levels of trust. (p. 21)

The guiding coalition should be made up of teachers and administrators who are eager to promote change, have teaching expertise, are credible and influential with their peers, and are proven leaders on campus (Kramer & Schuhl, 2017). Traits to avoid when selecting a guiding coalition are people with large egos, people who create mistrust and kill teamwork, and people who are wary of change (Spiller & Power, 2019). Figure 2.1 is a helpful template for determining and selecting who should and who should not be on the guiding coalition or leadership team. Administrators should seek to find teachers who maximize the four positive characteristics and avoid the negative traits.

As administrators are determining which teachers to ask to join the guiding coalition, they could ask for input from other teachers on campus or district colleagues and compile the information they gather using the leadership team selection protocol. Administrators should then invite those teachers they have selected to meet with them to discuss guiding coalition ongoing action items (discussed later in this chapter). Ideally, the team lead from each collaborative

Leadership Team Selection Protocol

Directions: Use the characteristics in each section to determine the most effective members of the leadership team.

Avoid (1) people with large egos, (2) people who create mistrust and kill teamwork, and (3) people who are wary of change (Spiller & Power, 2019).

Eagerness to Promote Change	**Expertise**
List individuals who are committed to school improvement.	List individuals who have demonstrated knowledge and experience that will support school improvement.
Credibility	**Leadership Skills**
List individuals who are influential among the other staff members.	List individuals who are proven leaders in the school.

Source: Kramer & Schuhl (2017), p. 10. Adapted from Buffum & Mattos (2014) and Kotter (1996); Spiller & Power (2019).
FIGURE 2.1: Leadership team selection protocol.
Visit go.SolutionTree.com/PLCbooks to download a free reproducible version of this figure.

team (for example, the grade 6 mathematics team) would be on the guiding coalition and some singletons as well, but only if those teachers meet the characteristics listed in figure 2.1.

It is also wise to spend the necessary time to get the guiding coalition enthusiastic about the goal of implementing the PLC process schoolwide. It is helpful to read articles and books about PLCs with the guiding coalition; consider bringing in a consultant to increase competence and confidence in the seven-step learning cycle and the rationale for the PLC Dashboard; and attend PLC Institutes. Two helpful readings to get started are the following:

- *The Futility of PLC Lite* by Richard DuFour and Douglas Reeves (2016)
- Pages 13–22 in *Learning by Doing, Fourth Edition* (DuFour et al., 2024; pages 9–17 in the third edition [DuFour et al., 2016])

Another way to generate enthusiasm is to visit a Model PLC school with your guiding coalition. As DuFour and colleagues (2024) explain, "Every Model PLC has effectively implemented all the essential elements of the PLC at Work process and has achieved multiple years of significant, sustained improvement in student achievement" (p. 9).

Visit **AllThingsPLC.info** (https://allthingsplc.info/evidence) to find schools like yours that have become Model PLCs by implementing the PLC process with success. The list of Model PLCs is searchable by school size, demographics, and location. Model PLC schools are typically eager to share what they know and have learned and will host visitors. I have also video conferenced with model PLC schools on several occasions as an alternative to site visits. These schools are a valuable resource when you want to see how PLC practices are being implemented in real schools.

Learn and Communicate PLC Fundamentals

Once the guiding coalition is established, members (along with the building principal or principals, who should also be members) can begin leading the PLC process. Effective guiding coalitions take the time to regularly learn together, including attending PLC trainings, reading books and articles, and visiting other model PLC schools, either virtually or in person. This learning will help guiding coalition members see the logic of a learning-focused mindset, discover how meaningful collaboration benefits students and teachers, and ensure each member is speaking similarly about the loose and tight elements in a PLC. After their collective learning, the guiding coalition should then begin teaching PLC fundamentals to the staff. PLC fundamentals they can teach include the following.

- Definition of a PLC
- Three big ideas of a PLC
- Four PLC critical questions
- Five tight elements in a PLC
- The seven-step learning cycle (explored in detail in this book in chapter 3, page 41)

Some leaders and teachers may feel they don't need a review of fundamental PLC concepts; however, let's be reminded of the words of DuFour and his colleagues (2024), which state, "Redundancy can be a powerful tool in effective communication, and we prefer redundancy to ambiguity" (p. 14). Since becoming a PLC is a strategy for improving student results, guiding coalitions ought to go back to the foundational definition of a true PLC to ensure all educators on campus are grounded in the fundamentals, even if it may feel redundant to some. DuFour and colleagues (2024) define a *professional learning community* as follows:

> An ongoing process in which educators work collaboratively in recurring cycles of collective inquiry and action research to achieve better results for the students they serve. (p. 14)

Keys aspects of the definition are as follows.

- **An ongoing process:** There is no finish line. It is a one-way road that is about continuous improvement.
- **Collaboratively:** Work is not done in isolation; rather, educators co-labor in teams.
- **Collective inquiry:** Educators inquire together what the standards expect and what students should learn as a result of each unit of study or course.
- **Action research:** Teachers must compare results to see what is working best, as teachers often utilize different instructional techniques.
- **Achieve better results for the students they serve:** The PLC process is not about what is easiest for the adults; in a PLC, adults do not "teach, test, and hope for the best!" as is common in traditional schools. In PLCs, the focus is on learning, rather than on teaching.

Consider using a quick ten-minute "learn together" portion of an upcoming staff meeting or even a short segment of a grade-level meeting where a member of the guiding coalition asks colleagues to define a PLC. Participants could then share their definitions with a shoulder partner, then share the actual definition, as well as the key aspects of the definition as listed previously. Wrap up the learning together by asking participants to share which aspects of the definition of a true PLC they think will positively impact students or their colleagues the most.

Three big ideas support the work in a PLC (DuFour et al., 2024).

1. **A focus on learning:** The school's focus isn't on teaching and covering the content; rather, the focus is on students learning what is deemed essential.

2. **A collaborative culture and collective responsibility:** Teachers work together to set goals for student proficiency for which they are mutually accountable. Isolation and competition are the opposites of this big idea.

3. **A focus on results:** The focus is not what the educators intended for students to learn. Instead, the focus is on outcomes, and if student results are not improving, then changes must be made to instruction, chosen essential learning targets, the rigor of common formative assessments, or intervention intensity.

Some educators mistakenly believe that any meeting at school could be called a PLC. However, a PLC is the larger organization, like a school or a district, in which educators work in collaborative teams in ongoing cycles of collective inquiry focusing on the four PLC critical questions (DuFour et al., 2024).

1. What do we want all students to learn and be able to do?
2. How will we know students have learned it?
3. What will we do when students haven't learned it?
4. What will we do when students have already learned it?

To reinforce the three big ideas and four critical questions, consider inserting another learning segment into an already existing staff gathering. You could start by asking participants to list the three big ideas or four critical questions and share their lists with a shoulder partner. After that, ask participants to rate which big ideas or critical questions are strengths for them and which could be improved.

There are five tight elements in a PLC (DuFour et al., 2024).

1. Work in collaborative teams rather than isolation.
2. Implement a guaranteed and viable curriculum, unit by unit.
3. Monitor student learning through team-developed common formative assessments.
4. Use assessment results to improve teaching practice.
5. Provide systematic interventions and extensions.

The five tight elements are not a list of actions for PLC schools to consider; they are required. When these tight elements are taught alongside the "loose" aspects of the process—those things with which educators have flexibility to implement as they see fit—educators can better understand the expectations and their roles and responsibilities.

In my study and implementation of the PLC fundamentals at the teacher, administrator, and consultant level, I identify two primary purposes of the PLC process.

1. Ensure all students learn the team- and singleton-determined essential learning targets.
2. Ensure teachers are learning new instructional strategies.

Too often, schools focus exclusively on the first purpose and neglect the second purpose. When this happens, educators are not professionals who are learning in a community, but merely teachers who are teaching in a community.

When teams and singletons work in collaborative teams, they work through the PLC process as detailed in the seven-step learning cycle, one essential learning target at a time, to facilitate both student and teacher learning. The guiding coalition needs to make clear what products teams and singletons are expected to produce, as there are several team products leaders will monitor and review. Those products are covered in greater detail in chapter 4 (page 79) and include such things as team norms, an annual listing of essential learning targets, common formative assessments, spreadsheets of student proficiency for each essential learning target, action plans for reteaching, interventions, and extensions, and changes to instructional strategies to make based on student results. While it may seem daunting to track all of these products for many teams, it is made easier when many of the expected products are combined into a simple, easy-to-follow template (described later in chapter 4) and monitored in The PLC Dashboard, as explained in chapter 5 (page 107).

Leaders and the guiding coalition have many resources at their disposal to provide staff with an overview of key PLC concepts and practices. Chapters 2 (page 23) and 3 (page 41) in this book provide an overview of key PLC concepts. After reading these chapters, discuss with the guiding coalition how to teach the concepts to the rest of the staff in settings that will facilitate the best discussions, and then make preliminary plans to do so. Teaching these concepts is often best accomplished in smaller groups, such as grade-level or departmental teams, instead of whole-staff meetings. Teaching PLC concepts can involve leading reading discussions (such as of influential segments from chapters 2 and 3 in this book, pages 18–21 in *Learning by Doing, Fourth Edition* (DuFour et al., 2024; or pages 11–14 in *Learning by Doing, Third Edition* [DuFour et al., 2016]), or other foundational PLC resources. A guiding coalition might have small groups of those in attendance jigsaw (break up the reading into chunks) the pertinent readings in this book or in *Learning by Doing* and then share out in small groups the two to three phrases that stood out the most to them from their chunk. During these meetings, guiding coalition members should engage colleagues in a discussion of the rationale of why becoming a PLC makes sense, the strategy of the seven-step learning cycle (chapter 3, page 41), and how to use the Essential Learning Target Plan (explained in chapter 4, page 79). In addition, the guiding coalition should assist the staff as they practice working through the templates and respond to staff concerns. After the guiding coalition has taught these PLC concepts to the rest of the staff, a good question for the guiding coalition leaders to ask teachers in this smaller-group setting is, "Are there any good reasons why we would not move forward with the PLC process?"

Determine Collaborative Teams and Singletons

The guiding coalition is also responsible for determining which teachers are on which collaborative teams, with the intention of making every team meaningful. Many schools have more than one teacher who teaches the same subject, but are they a collaborative team or just a group of people working near one another on a difficult and challenging task? DuFour and colleagues (2024) define a team as a group of people who "work interdependently to achieve a common goal for which members are mutually accountable" (p. 50). It is the *interdependence* of the *common goal* that differentiates groups from teams. For instance, marathon runners are working hard at the same goal in close proximity to one another, but nobody would call them a team, as the success or failure of any one runner has no impact on the others. However, in football, the entire team is accountable for the final score, not just the kicker many would like to blame who missed the last second field-goal attempt. Examples of meaningful teams within schools include two seventh-grade social studies teachers or the first-grade teachers.

Singletons are those teachers who do not have another course-alike teacher in the same building with whom to collaborate. Some schools have many singletons, but almost all schools have at least one. Some examples of singletons include the only band or physics teacher on campus, the departmentalized fifth-grade mathematics teacher at an elementary school, the middle school art teacher, or the only high school CTE auto mechanics teacher. Regretfully, too many singletons don't think the PLC process applies to them. Hattie (2015) reminds us, however, that "we must stop allowing teachers to work alone, behind closed doors and in isolation" (p. 23). The PLC process does apply to singletons who can make the shift from teaching to learning the essential learning targets (PLC big idea 1) and they should have a results orientation (big idea 3). However, their collaborative culture (big idea 2) just looks different.

Even those teachers who do not have a course-alike teammate in the same school need to find collaboration. In *Singletons in a PLC at Work*, authors Brig Leane and Jon Yost (2022) make the case that singletons must have collaboration that is meaningful to them, as isolation is the enemy of improvement.

The primary on-ramps for singletons to find meaningful collaboration (Leane & Yost, 2022) are as follows.

- **Course-alike on-ramp:** Teachers from different schools utilize technology to provide for virtual collaboration.
- **Common content on-ramp:** Teachers from the same school collaborate as a vertical team or by finding common skills.
- **Critical friend on-ramp:** Teachers from the same school who share a common collaboration time, but don't share any curriculum.

Figure 2.2 illustrates the three on-ramps.

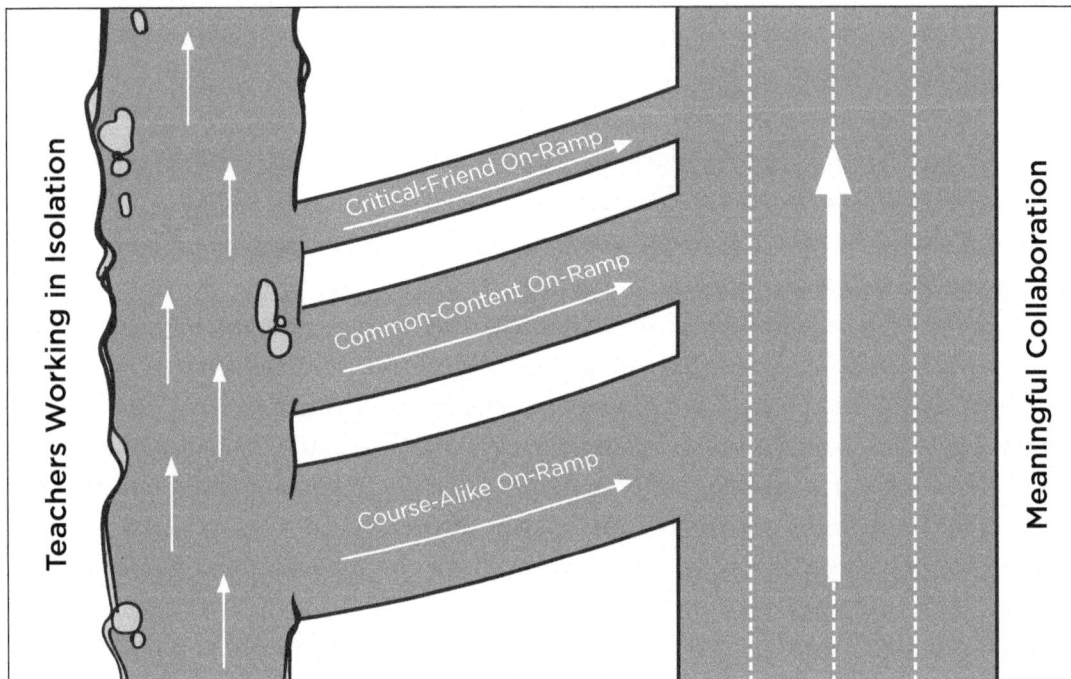

Source: Leane and Yost, 2022, p. 18.

FIGURE 2.2: The three on-ramps for collaboration for singletons.

Each teacher should be on only one team to begin with, even if they have multiple subjects they teach. For instance, a high school science teacher who teaches three classes of biology, one class of geology, and one class of AP chemistry might be best on the biology team. However, if only two science teachers teach geology, a geology team might be a better team organization as it would prevent the other geology teacher from working in isolation.

Special education teachers are sometimes mistakenly assigned to every team—a nearly impossible task of trying to be an active learning member with all teams. Consider making the special education teacher a member of one team that most of their caseload of students have in common; for instance, at an elementary school, the teacher could be assigned to the fourth-grade team, even if the special education teacher has a few students in other grades as well. This allows that teacher to be a contributing and learning member and to not be spread so thin that they cannot provide effective contributions to any team.

Each teacher on campus should be accounted for as either a member of a team or as a singleton in the first column of the PLC Dashboard.

Explain the Stages of Team Development

Often, after discussing the three big ideas and the four critical questions, administrators and educators are eager to get the PLC process started on campus. However, there is another consideration that I find to be particularly important to discuss and prepare for *prior to getting started*, and it is from the work of group dynamics researcher Bruce Tuckman. Tuckman (1965) and, later, Lynda Silsbee (2023) affirm the stages of team development to be (1) forming, (2) storming, (3) norming, and (4) performing.

Forming

In the *forming stage*, educators are learning what team they are on, learning about the PLC process, and examining what their team is going to be expected to produce. Teachers are usually polite, guarded, asking questions, and often somewhat intrigued by the work. I call this the *honeymoon stage*. Teams at this stage need clear expectations and guidance. They might begin establishing some basic norms such as what time they will meet, how they intend to handle disagreements, and how they will keep a student-focused learning orientation.

Storming

Quickly following the forming stage is the *storming stage* where there is resistance, opting out, competition, confronting one another, and general conflict. Emotions are high, and the honeymoon is over. When (not if) this stage happens, it will be important for everyone to have known about Tuckman's (1965) stages ahead of time. It is during the storming stage that teams will need to be reminded that storming is an expected part of the team-development process. Teams at this stage often need lots of support, including the presence of a coach or other leader to work alongside and help guide the team, especially if this stage lasts longer than a few meetings. Teams should be encouraged to add a few additional norms that might set how the team will run, provide further clarification of the exact time meetings start and end, and determine how decisions will be made. This is a stage to acknowledge conflicts and have norms to address those conflicts. If a member of the team can become the team leader, they can be extremely helpful in guiding the team through the storming stage.

Norming

Following the storming stage, teams that are developing begin *norming*. This will be a time when team norms will need to be reviewed again and adjusted so that teams can confront any issues that may be keeping the team from functioning well. This is the stage where issues, instead of people, are confronted by setting better team norms. Teams are getting organized as they start to understand the work that needs to be done during team meetings. Teams at this stage need feedback on the PLC products they create.

Performing

The last stage is *performing*, and this stage takes time to develop. This is where the system in place is working well, and the team is healthy. This does not mean that there is no conflict on the team, but rather that conflict is viewed as constructive, and the team is getting results. Teams at this stage need acknowledgment of their work and may need opportunities to observe other teams that are performing at an even higher level. Teams at this stage should be encouraged to solve problems together, but if unhealthy conflict arises, administrators may need to temporarily join the team to help seek win-win resolutions.

Members of the guiding coalition could present Tuckman's (1965) stages to the staff by showing the four stages on a screen, describing each stage, and asking teachers to discuss with someone near them what stage they believe their school is presently in. Several teachers could share which stage they think the school is in, and what they think the next stage will be like.

If educators are not aware of Tuckman's (1965) stages of team development prior to beginning their PLC journey, they might mistake the storms of change to be an indicator that a school is on the wrong pathway. A better interpretation of the storms that will occur on campus is that storms are normal, according to Tuckman; and storms are an indication that the team is developing. It seems to me that many good educational initiatives have ended prematurely simply because storms were misinterpreted to be an indication that the initiative wasn't working or that the school had chosen the wrong initiative. It would serve the school culture well if guiding coalitions would make Tuckman's stages of (normal) team development known throughout the school at an all-staff meeting and remind staff of the stages from time to time as a reminder of what to expect as teams develop. As they monitor the ongoing PLC process, the guiding coalition could ask teams to assess which of Tuckman's stages teachers think their team is in, why they think that, and what are the next steps the team should take to further team development.

Reiterate Team and Singleton Expectations

How does a school, district, or any organization know what is working or what needs to be changed? They do this by creating systems that monitor the most important aspects of the work being done. Author James Clear (2018) writes, "You do not rise to the level of your goals. You fall to the level of your systems. Your goal is your desired outcome. Your system is the collection of daily habits that will get you there" (p. 27). For a simple analogy, think of the sign-off sheets that are often in restaurant bathrooms. Restaurant managers don't want to get bad ratings or have dirty bathrooms, so some use sign-off sheets to help keep bathrooms clean. Similarly, school leaders do not want to overspend public money, so they have a system to track spending that will inform leaders of the spending status. Attendance rightfully matters to parents, teachers, and administrators, so systems are created to monitor student attendance in a timely manner. Most schools monitor their expenditures, student attendance, fire drills, and many other school functions, and yet the primary purpose of school is for students to learn, which begs the question: Is learning being monitored? I am not talking about grades and the communication of overall performance; rather, I am referring to the actual learning of the essential skills as identified by teachers, skill by skill and student by student. Too many educators cannot answer this question with specificity: *Are my students learning the essential skills?* Leaders must reiterate that teams and singletons will be working to be able to answer that question and that systems will be developed for that purpose.

Systems to monitor learning reduce the inequities that occur with varying teachers of the same grade level or subject, help ensure the most important things on campus are monitored, allow for scalability, and help busy administrators know which teams need more time and support. *Schools should create systems to monitor learning*—the very thing that matters most to the students you serve. In chapter 4, page 79, you will learn some easy-to-follow systems to get the process working well and ensure sustainability, culminating in the development of a PLC Dashboard.

As guiding coalitions are getting ready for the PLC journey, it is critical to ensure that teachers have time to collaborate, that support is offered when teams and singletons do not meet expectations, and that teachers are not already overloaded with too much on their plates. Let's look at each of these individually.

Time to Collaborate

Administrators must ensure teachers have consistent, designated time to collaborate. It is crucial that teachers have adequate time to do this work, ideally one hour per week during the regular school day for meeting as a collaborative team focused on the PLC process. If teachers do not have time, administrators should first create a plan to make the time for them to work together, as there is no reason to present this strategy and expect teachers to find time to collaborate on their own.

Support for Expectations

Administrators must also monitor and respond to individuals or teams that fail to fulfill PLC responsibilities, leaning more on the side of providing support before they expect and enforce accountability. They must also ensure new hires will fit well on established teams, and they must inundate the staff with positive and encouraging PLC stories. They will also have the lead responsibility for setting up and maintaining the PLC Dashboard (see chapter 5, page 107) to monitor team progress to know which teams need more time and support, and they should acknowledge and celebrate the many wins along the way.

I cannot overstate the importance of the principal's role: They simply must be involved in supporting expectations to ensure learning on campus.

Too Much Work

When schools are in the beginning stages of designing an implementation plan, an issue that often arises is that teachers feel they already have too much on their plates; as Eaker and Keating (2012) state, "Working hard and being tired is simply part of an educator's life" (p. 40). Since some educators on campus will feel this way, examining current expectations can be beneficial. I recommend an activity that helps give both teachers and administrators clarity about what exactly is on teachers' plates. It is as straightforward as it sounds and simply involves asking teachers to list everything they believe they are currently responsible for doing. This can start in groups of three or four and then expand so every teacher can see what other teachers together believe to be their responsibilities. This involves everything from lesson planning to answering emails to reviewing Individual Education Plans (IEPs) to completing report cards to making bulletin boards to taking attendance. I find that in some schools, teachers have expectations of themselves that administration doesn't have. In other places, administrators thought teachers should be doing something that teachers were unaware of. Just getting clarity about what is expected across the school is helpful not only to new teachers but also to experienced teachers who have come from other districts where expectations differed. Once the list of responsibilities has been created, administrators may look at one or more of the expectations listed and consider ways to take them off teachers' plates prior to adding one more thing. I am not suggesting that the PLC process is not worth it, but to ignore the often-overwhelming list of expectations already expected is foolish. Figure 2.3 helps you and your teams examine what is on teachers' plates.

"What's On Our Plates?" Activity Guide

Materials, Activity Steps, and Discussion Questions

Materials needed: Notecards or sticky notes, sheets of paper, pens, poster paper, and markers

Steps to take:

1. Have teachers sit in groups of three or four.

2. Ask, "On one piece of paper, list the things your group believes you are responsible for at school." Give groups five or six minutes to complete their list. You can start this activity by having teachers individually list what they believe is on their plate on notecards or sticky notes prior to discussing it with colleagues.

3. With a scribe ready to record group lists, create a list on poster paper of responsibilities as groups call out what they wrote.

4. Put checks by items that have been listed more than once.

5. Ask, "Is anything missing from this list?"

6. Circle items that are required to be done by law or board policy.

7. Have groups discuss what they notice about the list on the poster paper.

8. Take the poster paper to the next guiding coalition meeting to determine what can be removed from teachers' plates.

9. Discuss the decisions that have been made with teachers.

FIGURE 2.3: "What's on our plates?" activity guide.

*Visit **go.SolutionTree.com/PLCbooks** to download a free reproducible version of this figure.*

Monitor the Work of Teams and Singletons

Forming a guiding coalition at the beginning of this journey provides the entire school with more effective and dispersed guidance, support, unity, and encouragement as staff members learn together through the PLC process. The next step is to monitor the work of teams. The guiding coalition will primarily monitor the following tasks.

1. Set the minimum number of essential learning targets (ELTs) for teams and singletons.

2. Monitor student learning of the essential learning targets through the PLC Dashboard (described in detail in chapter 5, page 107).

3. Provide feedback on and share exemplary PLC team products with staff.

Set the Minimum Number of Essential Learning Targets

After assigning the collaborative teams and beginning to teach the PLC process, the guiding coalition can set the *minimum* number of essential learning targets on which each collaborative team and singleton is required to work through the PLC process in a school year. For instance, the guiding coalition could start by saying that every team will aim to get through the process a minimum of once per month, or three to four times within a semester. This would equate to a minimum of eight or nine essential learning targets in the school year. When starting out, it is more important to go through the process thoroughly with fewer essential learning targets than to have too many essential learning targets and not get the process right. Teachers are already working hard, and just like early and late adopters of new technologies, some teams will be able to work efficiently through the cycle right away while others will need more time and support.

I typically aim to get teams that have been doing this process for a year or two into a rhythm of collaborating through the seven-step learning cycle approximately every three weeks. This would mean that each team or singleton would have approximately twelve essential learning targets for a year-long class. Those twelve essential learning targets become the guaranteed and viable curriculum and can be increased as teams get better at the process over time. The key is to find the sweet spot where teams have neither too many essential learning targets nor too few and ensure that the essential learning targets teams have selected are producing results.

Remember that the Essential Learning Targets are not all that teachers are going to teach. The essential learning targets represent the few learnings that are so important that teachers will do all they can to ensure learning of those, including reteaching interventions, regardless of the teacher to whom a student is assigned. Teachers will teach, assess, and grade many other concepts and skills, but with limited collaboration time, the essential learning targets are the basis for teachers learning from each other, as they co-labor to ensure students learn them as well. An effective guiding coalition will make this minimum expectation known to the staff after deciding together what the minimum number should be.

Especially when schools are beginning this process, I want to be clear that the number of essential learning targets that go through the seven-step learning cycle is most likely smaller than the number of essential learning targets the teachers believe students really need within a school year. And that number of essential learning targets is smaller than the total number of standards for the subject or grade level. Simply stated, the essential learning targets that go through the seven-step learning cycle are the specific knowledge, skills, and dispositions students must know and be able to do. Students who are not initially proficient in these skills will receive in-class reteaching as well as subsequent team-determined (Tier 2) interventions, and student growth and achievement on these skills will be the basis for teachers learning from one another what is working best. The list of essential learning targets to meet both purposes must be doable (viable).

An effective way to begin is by having all teams and singletons select one essential learning target for students to learn within the next month of school. Often this feels very doable, especially when this process is started during the school year.

Monitor Student and Teacher Learning With Each Essential Learning Target

Since learning is the primary purpose of school, it must be monitored. Effective guiding coalitions examine interim and end-of-year assessment results to determine how the PLC process is impacting student results. This gives educators tangible proof that their efforts are making an impact, and it also helps the school target areas that still need improvement. In addition, during guiding coalitions meetings, members should review the PLC Dashboard, as detailed in chapter 5 (page 107). Teachers should also be expected to have a visual in their classrooms of the current essential learning target, as well as the overall current percent proficiency of students at meeting it. For secondary schools, this is often broken up by class period. An example is shown in figure 2.4.

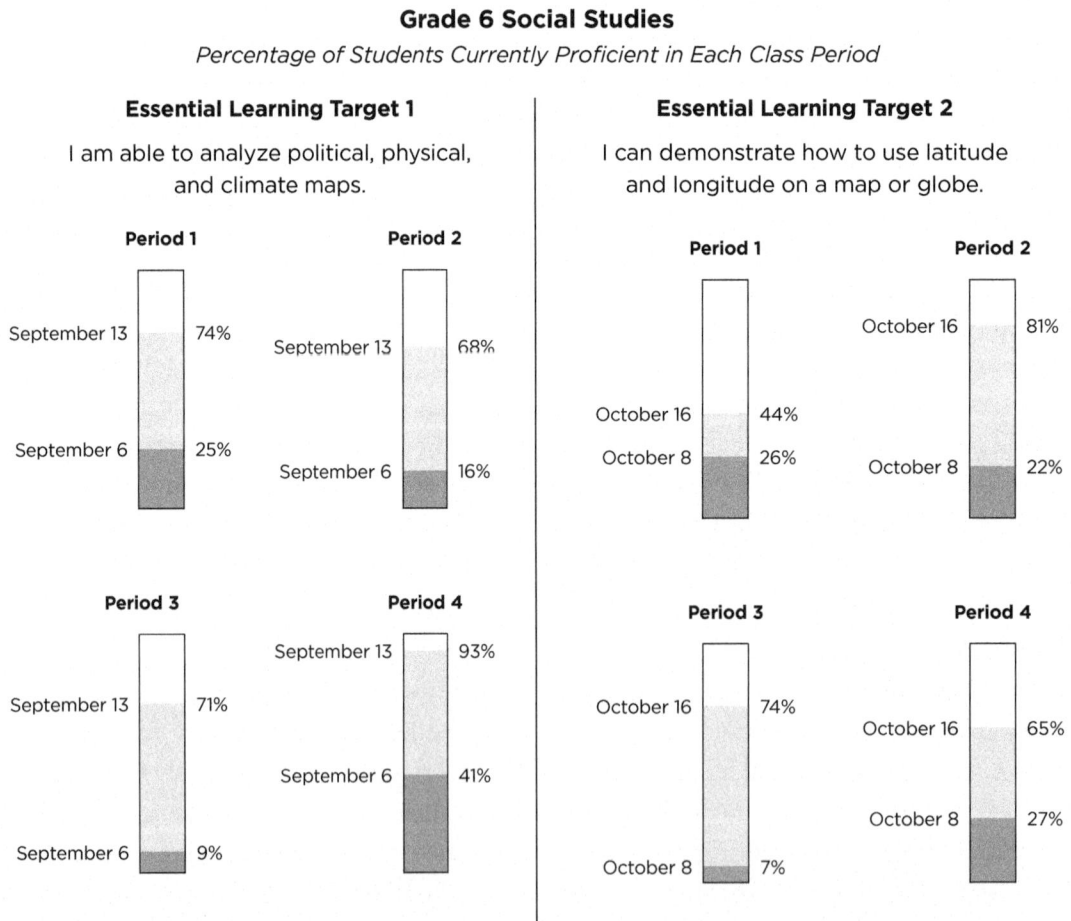

Grade 6 Social Studies
Percentage of Students Currently Proficient in Each Class Period

Essential Learning Target 1

I am able to analyze political, physical, and climate maps.

Period 1	Period 2
September 13 — 74%	September 13 — 68%
September 6 — 25%	September 6 — 16%

Period 3	Period 4
September 13 — 71%	September 13 — 93%
	September 6 — 41%
September 6 — 9%	

Essential Learning Target 2

I can demonstrate how to use latitude and longitude on a map or globe.

Period 1	Period 2
October 16 — 44%	October 16 — 81%
October 8 — 26%	October 8 — 22%

Period 3	Period 4
October 16 — 74%	October 16 — 65%
	October 8 — 27%
October 8 — 7%	

FIGURE 2.4: Classroom visual of student proficiency.

Use the checklist in figure 2.5 to ensure readiness for teams and singletons to work through the seven-step learning cycle. Note: Not everything in the checklist in figure 2.5 is covered in this chapter, like the details of the seven-step learning cycle, which are covered in chapter 3 (page 41).

Provide Feedback and Share

Through the review and feedback process, the guiding coalition shares exemplary aspects of Essential Learning Target Plans (detailed in chapter 4, page 79) with the rest of the staff to help teams and singletons grow in their understanding of the expectations. Teams need feedback on their products. This crucial guiding coalition support will be discussed in more detail in chapter 4 (page 79).

Are We Ready?

Directions: Use the following checklist as a guiding coalition to determine if your school is ready for teams and singletons to begin working through the seven-step learning cycle.

☐ We created a guiding coalition of administrators and teacher leaders.

☐ We taught PLC fundamentals to all teachers.

☐ We explained Tuckman's (1965) stages of team development to all teachers.

☐ We listed team and singleton expectations.

☐ We ensured teams and singletons have approximately one hour per week to focus on the seven-step learning cycle.

☐ We conducted the "What's on our Plates?" activity.

☐ We determined which teachers are on which teams and who are the singletons.

☐ We set the minimum number of essential learning targets for teams and singletons within an upcoming amount of time, such as the first quarter of the school year or the upcoming semester.

☐ We ensured singletons understand the three on-ramps for them to move from working in isolation to finding meaningful collaboration.

☐ We prepared a method to give teams and singletons meaningful feedback on their Essential Learning Target Plans.

☐ We set expectations and showed examples of how teachers could visually display the essential learning target progress of students in classrooms.

☐ We ensured each team has created and submitted a list of norms.

☐ We scheduled time for administrators to join teams at least once every three weeks to support them.

☐ We determined when and what celebrations will take place.

☐ We created a schedule for the guiding coalition to meet at least every two weeks.

FIGURE 2.5: Are we ready? checklist.

*Visit **go.SolutionTree.com/PLCbooks** to download a free reproducible version of this figure.*

Summary

Getting ready to implement the PLC process by selecting the right teacher leaders to be a part of the guiding coalition, learning and communicating PLC fundamentals, determining collaborative teams and singletons, explaining the stages of team development, reiterating team and singleton expectations, and setting up expectations and procedures for monitoring the work of teams and singletons will ensure your school is set up for success when teams and singletons begin their work on the seven-step learning cycle, which is covered in the next chapter.

Take a moment to pause and reflect on your current situation after reading this chapter. What evidence do you have that you are getting PLC implementation right, and what evidence do you have that you aren't there yet? After reflecting, explore the suggested resources for further study individually or with your teams.

PAUSE AND REFLECT

Evidence you are getting it right:

- You have established a respected guiding coalition that is eager for positive change across the campus.

- The guiding coalition has ensured staff members have learned PLC fundamentals.

- Every teacher is on a team or identified as a singleton.

- Teachers know that storms will be coming as one of the stages of development.

- Teachers have time during the contractual day to focus on the four critical questions of learning.

- The guiding coalition has set the minimum number of essential learning targets for teams and singletons.

- Teachers understand how to implement a visual in their classrooms of the current essential learning target, including some way to tell overall proficiency.

Evidence you aren't there yet:

- The guiding coalition is made up of volunteers.

- There is an assumption that everyone already knows and remembers all PLC fundamentals.

- Some teachers are expected to be on multiple teams at once.

- The guiding coalition doesn't think storms will happen as this change process takes place.

- Teachers have too much on their plates to add anything else; the guiding coalition doesn't take away anything to make room for this work.

- There is no clarity on how many times teams and singletons are expected to get through the PLC process.

- There is no evidence in classrooms of how students are doing collectively on an essential skill or evidence is not kept up to date.

What is a strength from this step that may already be going well on campus that you could acknowledge and celebrate?

RESOURCES FOR FURTHER STUDY

- Chapter 3 of *Leading With Intention: Eight Areas for Reflection and Planning in Your PLC at Work®* by Jeanne Spiller and Karen Power (2019)

- Chapters 1 and 2 of *Learning by Doing* by Richard DuFour, Rebecca DuFour, Robert Eaker, Thomas W. Many, Mike Mattos, and Anthony Muhammad (2024)

- Chapter 1 of *Powerful Guiding Coalitions: How to Build and Sustain the Leadership Team in Your PLC at Work®* by Bill Hall (2022)

3

Implementing the Seven-Step Learning Cycle

Passion alone can't cut it. For passion to survive it needs structure.
A why without how has little probability of success.

—SIMON SINEK

As a middle school principal, I was frustrated when I wanted our school to follow the PLC process, but I didn't have clarity on how to work through the process or the products that would guide it. I don't want other educators to spin their wheels like I did, as clarity can bring focus and efficiency. We wouldn't expect students to hit a learning target they can't see—why would we expect teachers to be able to implement strategies and processes that aren't as clear as possible?

While working with teachers across the United States, I often hear the question, "We believe in the PLC process, but where does our team start?" These educators don't know "how to PLC." I have seen several PLC process flowcharts, many of which were influential to me as a teacher, an administrator, and now as a consultant. The PLC process at the team level is also woven throughout landmark books such as *Learning by Doing* (DuFour et al., 2024) and *Revisiting Professional Learning Communities at Work, Second Edition* (DuFour, DuFour, Eaker, Mattos, & Muhammad, 2021). Out of my desire to meet the needs of the teams I coach, I asked myself, In addition to these and other foundational PLC books, what else do teams need to do this work effectively? I began to develop some simple how-to steps to share with educators who wanted more clarity about how to follow the PLC process reliably and efficiently. The seven-step learning cycle can be captured in the Essential Learning Target Plan (ELTP, introduced in chapter 4, page 79), which is integrated into the PLC Dashboard. As PLC author and consultant Brandon Jones says, *process* leads to *products*, which lead to *progress*. Likewise, the seven-step learning cycle leads to the Essential Learning Target Plan, which leads to the PLC Dashboard, which leads to sustained results.

The Seven-Step Learning Cycle

For those who have already started the PLC process, you may have become stalled or gotten off track. If so, you can easily "hit reset" by reviewing the seven steps to determine how to get back on track. Maybe your continued success is just a matter of bolstering some of your processes to solidify a particular step, or perhaps starting from step one will give your school the clarity it needs for successful implementation. The seven steps will guide your teams with clarity on the exact work to be done to become high-performing collaborative teams in a PLC as students learn the essential learning and adults learn from one another.

The seven-step learning cycle is made up of the following steps.

1. Determine the essential learning target.
2. Set a SMART goal and create the common formative assessment.
3. Give the common formative assessment.
4. Ensure inter-rater reliability.
5. Share results.
6. Develop and implement an action plan for intervention and extension.
7. Capture team learning and make changes to instruction.

The seven-step cycle is shown in figure 3.1.

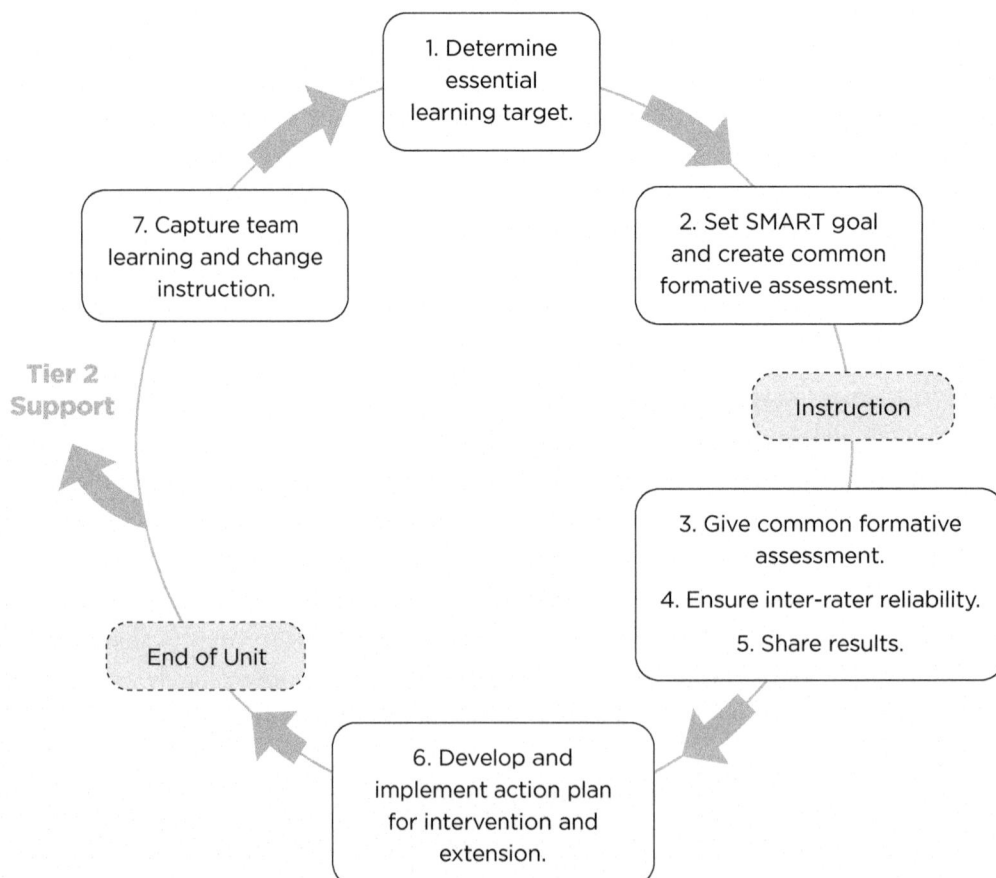

FIGURE 3.1: The seven-step learning cycle.

The two shaded boxes in figure 3.1 indicate when the steps in the cycle happen in relation to the teaching within a unit, as well as where intervention and extension happen in relation to the end of a unit of study. Too often, educators wait until a unit is over to intervene with struggling learners. Intervention should begin after giving common formative assessments and before a unit is over.

Teachers need to teach many concepts and skills over the course of a school year. They might have a curriculum to guide them, and teachers most likely have standards to meet. The obvious goal of teaching is for students to learn, and the seven-step learning cycle helps teams ensure learning for all, both students and teachers. However, when teachers have dozens of standards to meet, it is not reasonable or possible to get every student to proficiency in all the standards to the level that the seven-step learning cycle ensures. In a PLC, teams use the seven-step learning cycle for a carefully selected portion of the knowledge, skills, and dispositions that students must know—the essential learning targets. Everything else teachers teach is considered "nice to know" from the perspective of the PLC process.

Teams work through the seven-step learning cycle collaboratively. As discussed in chapter 2 (page 23), many schools have singletons who might not be part of grade- or subject-level teams or vertical teams. My hope is that singleton teachers find a meaningful collaborative partner. Singletons using the course-alike and common content on-ramps (see chapter 2) will go through the seven-step learning cycle as shown in figure 3.1. However, singletons who have not yet found a meaningful collaborative partner, including those using the critical friend on-ramp (see chapter 2) should use the altered learning cycle shown in figure 3.2.

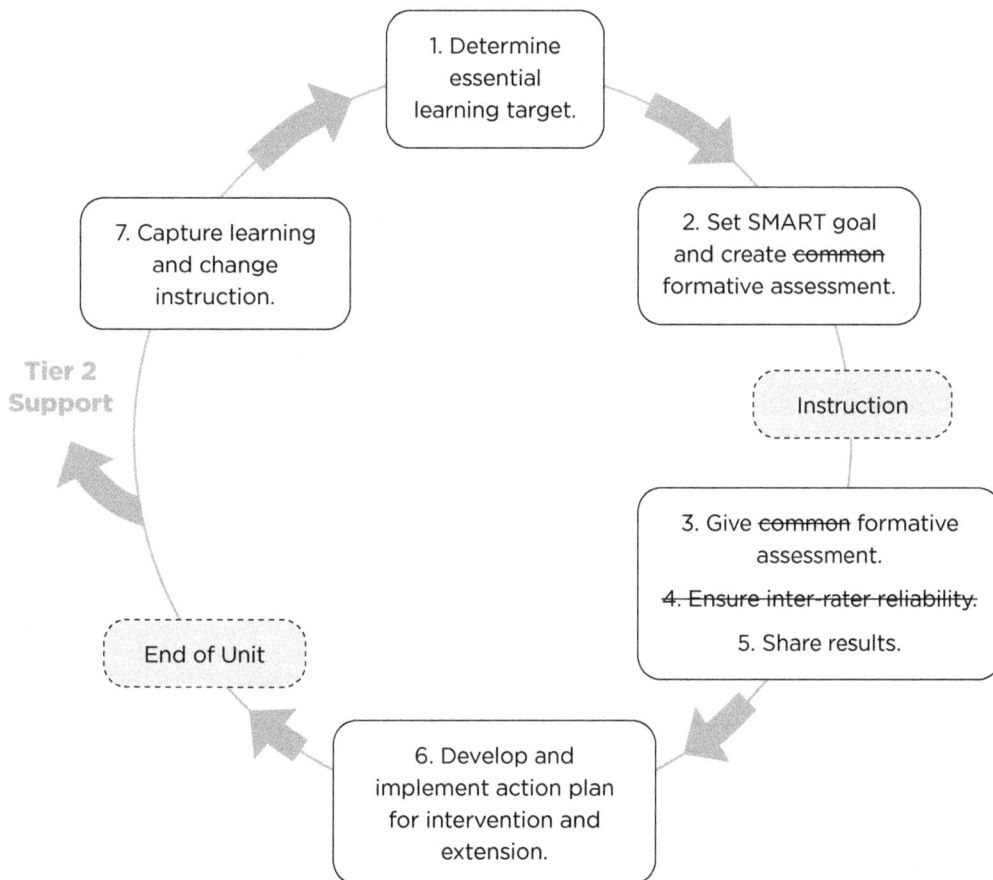

FIGURE 3.2: The adapted learning cycle with changes for isolated singletons.

The sections that follow guide you through the thinking behind each step. An indication that teams are doing it right is if they are focusing on one or more steps of the seven-step learning cycle per team meeting. If a team is discussing topics unrelated to any of the seven steps, that is an indication that they are using their limited team time for the wrong purposes. While there are many other topics teachers may need to discuss that are not associated with any of the seven steps, collaborative team time is limited and should focus only on one or more of the seven steps. During some meetings, a team might complete one step or even a few, but generally, it takes a team about three weeks of meeting approximately one hour per week to get through all the steps, with some of the work being completed outside of designated team time.

Step 1: Determine the Essential Learning Target

If we were to take a trip, the first question most would ask is, "Where are we going?" It is not worth discussing the route we should take before we determine the destination. It is the same for collaborative teams and singletons in a PLC; the destination is what teachers want all students to learn in an upcoming unit of study, and the routes are the various learning activities and instructional strategies they will use. The first critical question collaborative teams in a PLC ask is, "What do we want students to know and be able to do?" (DuFour et al., 2024, p. 44) in a certain amount of time. Education and PLC experts Mike Mattos, Austin Buffum, and Janet Malone (2018) state, "If we are to build a solid foundation of essential skills and knowledge in students . . . we must be crystal clear what those skills and knowledge are" (p. 84). Teams should identify these skills, the essential learning targets (ELTs), at least before a unit of study begins, but this step can also be done before a school year begins.

Determining essential learning targets can be broken down into two substeps.

1. Prioritize the standards.
2. Unpack a prioritized standard into learning targets.

When considering standards, teachers will separate what is essential from what is simply nice to know within a unit of study. Collaborative team time will focus on ensuring students learn the essential learning targets. The nice-to-know material may still be taught either as an extension or during regular class time and included in grading, but teams will not go through the seven-step learning cycle for this material. As a collaborative team, or as a singleton, teachers will also have to determine the material they are willing to sacrifice, as there usually isn't time to cover every lesson in the curriculum. Experts note that students can't adequately learn everything expected in the standards in the amount of time allotted (DuFour & Marzano, 2011).

While some districts want a team of teachers to handle the selection of the essential learning targets for an entire district, this work must be done at the collaborative team level to maximize its effectiveness. In the book *The Seven Habits of Highly Effective People*, author Stephen Covey (1989) emphasizes that "without involvement, there is no commitment" (p. 143). For collaborative teams and singletons to have the internal drive necessary to complete the seven-step cycle, including multiple interventions if needed, teachers simply must be committed to the essential learning targets, and their involvement in choosing those themselves helps create that commitment. If the essential learning targets are handed down from any other level, including the state, province, district, textbook, principal, or another teacher team, teachers could easily forego the challenges of the process and feel justified saying, "I didn't think that essential learning target was very important, anyway."

While it is critical that teams and singletons determine the essential learning targets for themselves, it is extremely helpful for districts to narrow the standards down to *district priority standards* or *district power standards*. When districts narrow the standards, these smaller lists can then become the set of standards from which teams and singletons choose their essential learning targets. Teachers are usually tasked with "covering" all the standards. But there is only so much time available, so teachers must focus on the essential learning targets that come from essential standards.

Prioritize the Standards

How do teams and singletons determine what all students must learn in a unit of study? The standards are the best place to start, as the standards represent what each state or province has determined educators must teach. Teachers can simply list the standards from the next unit and rank them from most to least important, using the R.E.A.L. criteria (Ainsworth, 2013). These are the guiding questions collaborative team members should ask one another when considering a standard.

1. **Readiness: Does the standard develop student readiness for the next level of learning?** Is it essential for success in the next unit, course, or grade level?

2. **Endurance: Does the standard have endurance?** Do we really expect students to retain the knowledge and skills over time as opposed to merely learning it for a test?

3. **Assessed: Is the standard assessed?** Will the standard be assessed on state tests, college entrance tests, military entrance tests, or trade school tests?

4. **Leverage: Does the standard have leverage?** Will proficiency in this standard help the student in other areas of the curriculum and other academic disciplines? (Ainsworth, 2013)

The R.E.A.L. criteria help team members to be objective when assessing what is essential.

I recall a particular team I was working with that was beginning to determine essential learning targets in a mathematics unit. One member of the team thought it was important for students to know the names of famous historical mathematicians and their contributions to modern mathematics. The other teachers believed that it was more important for students to be proficient in using proportions to solve specific problems. The R.E.A.L. criteria gave the teammates questions to ask and discuss. When asked how knowledge of mathematicians would develop readiness for the next level of learning, the team member agreed it did not. The knowledge of mathematicians also wasn't enduring, as most of the team knew very little about any of the mathematicians, so the students wouldn't need to retain this information either. In addition, the knowledge of mathematicians wasn't in the standards, and it would not be in any future assessments outside of the one teacher's class. By reviewing the R.E.A.L.

criteria, the team determined that knowing mathematicians was not essential; however, if time permitted, teachers could still teach that information.

Figure 3.3 is a tool teams can use to determine which priority standards are essential. The sample shows the work of a seventh-grade mathematics team. Visit **go.SolutionTree.com /PLCbooks** to download a blank reproducible version of this template.

Alternatively, teams might use their intended curriculum to determine the essential learning in a unit. They might also review prior lesson plans to see what they decided was essential in previous years, or at other times when the team prioritized essential learning because of time or logistical constraints.

Sometimes teams might want to discuss a disposition they want every student to have that might not come from a standard. For instance, a team or singleton might want every student to be able to demonstrate grit, digital citizenship, or make an effective presentation. The seven-step learning cycle is intended for academic skills, but it can also be used to discuss knowledge or dispositions that might not come from an identifiable standard.

Grade-level teams at the elementary level could choose one subject area as an initial focus, unless the guiding coalition decides that data in a particular subject area show it needs the most improvement across the school. For instance, an elementary school might choose mathematics as a focus subject and go through the seven-step learning cycle with that subject for the first year and then add other subjects as the teachers grow more familiar with the cycle over time.

Additionally, secondary teachers with multiple subjects need to keep the work manageable. I recommend selecting one subject or class to focus on at first and then expanding as capacity for this work grows.

Perhaps teachers already know what students should learn in their courses based on prior experience with the curriculum. In that case, teachers can select one of those skills that is coming up next in the curriculum and find the standard that fits. In this instance, teachers wouldn't be prioritizing the skill against all the other standards; rather, they would need to be confident they are selecting a high-value (essential) standard.

Regardless of where collaborative teams and singletons find the skills to consider as essential learning targets, I will refer to them as *standards* for simplicity, as that is primarily where essential learning targets should come from. Teams and singletons will need to prioritize standards as a way of getting to the most important targets, and a useful guide for accomplishing this is to apply the R.E.A.L. criteria.

After analyzing each standard from the unit using the R.E.A.L. criteria, teams rank them from most to least important, with those with four yes answers qualifying as most important. The standards ranked at the top of the list now become eligible to be taken through the next step of unpacking the standard. The teams that picked one standard and confirmed it as high value are also ready to move on to unpacking it.

Unpack a Prioritized Standard Into Learning Targets

The goal of unpacking a standard is to get familiar with the rigor of the standard and determine the learning target or targets deemed most critical within that standard. Some also refer to this process as unwrapping or deconstructing standards. Several effective methods

Priority Standard	Readiness	Endurance	Assessed	Leverage
7.RP.A.1: Compute unit rates associated with ratios of fractions, including ratios of lengths, areas and other quantities measured in like or different units.	X	X	X	X
7.RP.A.2: Recognize and represent proportional relationships between quantities.	X	X	X	X
7.NS.A.3: Solve real-world and mathematical problems involving the four operations with rational numbers.	X	X	X	X
7.EE.A.1: Apply properties of operations as strategies to add, subtract, factor, and expand linear expressions with rational coefficients.	X			
7.EE.B.3: Solve multistep real-life and mathematical problems posed with positive and negative rational numbers in any form (whole numbers, fractions, and decimals), using tools strategically.	X	X	X	X
7.EE.B.4: Use variables to represent quantities in a real-world or mathematical problem, and construct simple equations and inequalities to solve problems by reasoning about the quantities.	X		X	X
7.G.A.2: Draw (freehand, with ruler and protractor, and with technology) geometric shapes with given conditions.				
7.G.A.3: Describe the two-dimensional figures that result from slicing three-dimensional figures, as in plane sections of right rectangular prisms and right rectangular pyramids.				
7.G.B.4: Know the formulas for the area and circumference of a circle and use them to solve problems; give an informal derivation of the relationship between the circumference and area of a circle.	X		X	
7.SP.A.1: Understand that statistics can be used to gain information about a population by examining a sample of the population.	X	X	X	X
7.SP.C.5: Understand that the probability of a chance event is a number between 0 and 1 that expresses the likelihood of the event occurring.	X		X	
7.SP.C.8: Find probabilities of compound events using organized lists, tables, tree diagrams, and simulation.			X	

Source for standards: National Governors Association Center for Best Practices & Council of Chief State School Officers, 2010.

FIGURE 3.3: Grade 7 mathematics team sample for identifying essential standards.

*Visit **go.SolutionTree.com/PLCbooks** to download a free reproducible version of this figure.*

exist that detail this process, including an effective unpacking template in *School Improvement for All* (Kramer & Schuhl, 2017; see page 71) and more detailed steps in *Simplifying Common Assessment: A Guide for Professional Learning Communities at Work* (Bailey & Jakicic, 2017; see pages 21–27). If you are an instructional coach, are really struggling with unpacking standards, or want more depth of insight into this process, I recommend referring to one of these other resources, but if you have unpacked standards before, the six-step method I recommend is user-friendly. A template for teams and singletons to use to unpack standards appears in figure 3.4.

1. Write the essential standard.

2. Determine the prerequisite skills students need to know and the vocabulary that teachers should explicitly teach to students.

3. List a few reasons why knowing the standard is relevant in the life of a student. Ask and answer overarching questions about the standard, such as "Why would students and adults want to be able to tell the difference between fact and opinion?" or "What aspects of everyday life require proportional thinking?" This ensures clarity across the team of why the chosen standard is important to know, which teachers will then emphasize to students throughout the unit of study.

4. Break the standard into "I can . . ." statements that together make up the standard. These statements should be written at the rigor (depth of knowledge) of the standard by using the same verbs as those contained in the standard. Determine the essential *I can* statement from the nice-to-know statements. Circle the essential *I can* statement—this is now the essential learning target. The circled essential learning target will go through the remaining six steps of the seven-step learning cycle. When going through the cycle for the first few times, it is best to start with just one essential learning target per unit (except for units that span months).

5. Begin to develop the common formative assessment to answer the question, "How would a student demonstrate proficiency of that essential learning target?"

6. List any research-based or other effective instructional strategies that teachers should use to teach the circled essential learning target or targets.

The team then adds the unpacked essential learning target to their list of annual essential learning targets. The team can make this list as the school year progresses or do the work to compile it prior to the beginning of the school year. Over time, the list of essential learning targets become the guaranteed and viable curriculum. Teams record each essential learning target in the Team and Singleton Information tab in the PLC Dashboard (see chapter 5, page 107). The team will eventually record student learning of that essential learning target in one of columns F–I of the PLC Dashboard, where teams and leaders look to monitor student learning and the teams' work. The essential learning target will be recorded in the Essential Learning Target Plan as discussed in chapter 4 (page 79).

As teachers plan for each unit, they repeat this unpacking process for another prioritized standard from the next unit. The key is to keep the seven-step learning cycle ongoing and sustainable—a balance that usually has experienced teams and singletons going through the cycle about every three to four weeks.

Essential Standards Unpacking Template

What knowledge, skill, or disposition does every student need to know or be able to do? (DuFour et al., 2024)

Purpose: Use this template to unpack essential standards that meet the REAL criteria: readiness, endurance, assessed, and leverage.

Step 1: Write the essential standard to unpack.

HAS-REI.C.6: Solve systems of linear equations exactly and approximately (e.g. with graphs), focusing on pairs of linear equations in two variables.

Step 2: List the prerequisite skills the standard requires and the vocabulary to teach.

Prerequisite skills: Solving a multistep equation, graphing a linear equation, fraction multiplication, signed number operations, order of operations, plotting points, creating input-output tables from equations

Vocabulary to teach: Linear equation, intersection, solution, system, variables, coordinate plane, approximate

---

Step 3: List the reasons why knowing this standard is relevant for students and how you will make those reasons known to them.

When two different companies have different cost structures, such as one plumbing company offering an hourly rate and another offering a flat fee, this helps consumers know the advantages and disadvantages of the different options.

This is used in business to determine when a company will make a profit and also useful in investing to determine which investment is best.

Step 4: List the *I can* statements that describe what a proficient student could do to meet the essential standard and the rigor (depth of knowledge) expected. (Use the same verbs as in the standard.)

I can solve a system of two linear equations and approximate where they intersect by graphing. (DOK 2)

I can solve a system of two linear equations and determine where they intersect without graphing them. (DOK 2)

Step 5: Circle the *I can* statements from step 4 that are essential and will be in the formative assessment (most likely not all of them). Include examples here of the questions students will be asked on the formative assessment to show the rigor of the essential learning targets.

Solve this system of linear equations by graphing. Determine the approximate location of the intersection. $y = \frac{1}{2}x + 7$ and $y = -3x + 1$

Step 6: List any strategies that teachers should use to teach the circled essential learning targets.

Dry-erase practice boards of graphing lines, input-output tables to plot points, and Kagan cooperative groups

---

FIGURE 3.4: Essential standards unpacking template.

*Visit **go.SolutionTree.com/PLCbooks** to download a free reproducible version of this figure.*

One final note: Teachers do not need to unpack each standard every year if the essential learning targets stay the same. Teams and singletons should perform this step only when considering a new standard as a priority. This would occur when teacher teams have determined that the essential learning targets they have selected are not getting the expected results on other measures, such as standardized interim or year-end assessments, or when a new team member joins a team and would like to consider a new standard. Teachers should plan to keep completed Essential Standards Unpacking Templates to refer to each year. The six remaining steps of the cycle flow directly from the unpacking process, as the essential learning targets from unpacking become the basis for the SMART goal, the common formative assessment, the action plan, and the focus of educators' professional development for the unit.

Determine How Many Essential Learning Targets Fit Into a School Year

Using the guiding coalition's minimum number as a starting point, the number of essential learning targets teams and singletons select over the course of an entire school year must be reasonable. Remember, all the standards may be taught, but only the selected essential learning targets will go through the seven-step learning cycle (be assessed and involve intervention) to be *learned* by all students. I find most teams and singletons in the first few years of the cycle have between eight to twelve essential learning targets per year. Simply put, experienced teams should work to become able to get through the seven-step learning cycle approximately every three to four weeks. This applies to elementary teachers who may have students all day, as well as to secondary teachers who only see the same students one period a day.

It is best principals do not decide the specific number of essential learning targets but instead allow collaborative teams and singletons to decide the number (following the guiding coalition's required minimum) and rigor of essential learning targets that would strongly correlate to proficiency in the grade level or subject for that year. If the number is too high, teachers could become exasperated. If the number is too low, teachers could have idle time where valuable collaboration time is not maximized.

Some educators may want to put many more Essential Learning Targets through the seven-step learning cycle. While this is rarely a problem, it is important that teams and singletons do not have so many essential learning targets that each one becomes a tiny step completed in a short amount of time, where tracking student progress, intervening, and capturing team learning become overwhelming.

Some teacher teams may only be able to take six identified essential learning targets through the complete seven-step learning cycle the first year. The number of times a team works through the cycle is not as important as keeping teams engaged in the process with the time they have to collaborate without being overwhelmed. As long as teams are making progress in the cycle, I recommend principals adapt expectations to team needs, increasing expectations as team capacity to handle the process grows.

Reach Consensus

If a team cannot come to consensus on an essential learning target within a unit of study, the team needs immediate assistance, as determining an essential learning target must take place for the team to move forward with the cycle. Teams that think they need to pick the perfect essential learning target should be relieved to know that lists of essential learning targets are not carved in stone. Even if a poorly determined essential learning target is selected, the ongoing seven-step learning cycle will eventually work to correct that as well. The test of whether a team is choosing essential learning targets wisely comes when schools get student results back from broader summative assessments, such as state or district benchmark assessments. This will help the team determine if proficiency on the essential learning target they picked was a good indicator of proficiency in the overall subject. From these results, teams can adjust the essential learning target list as needed.

To assist teams and singletons that are stuck, administrators or instructional coaches should join those teams each time they meet. Administrators or instructional coaches could bring a list of standards to prioritize or ask teams more probing questions about each standard they are unpacking. You will need to be loose about what teams pick as an essential learning target, but you will need to be tight that they do choose—choosing essential learning targets is a non-negotiable. Helping educators find additional time to do this work is also critical. This is addressed further in chapter 4 (page 79).

Even if a singleton couldn't see how any of the three on-ramps mentioned in chapter 2 (page 23) could work for them, there is still work to be done for the singleton preparing to be a future meaningful collaborative teammate (Leane & Yost, 2022). Thinking back to the seven-step learning cycle, could a singleton still determine in step 1 an essential learning target that every student should know and be able to do? The answer is yes.

Make Essential Learning Targets Clear to Students and Parents

Once teams and singletons have determined the essential learning target in a unit of study, that target needs to be made clear to students and parents. This can be done at back-to-school events and posted on class websites and should be done for each unit of study.

In addition, one schoolwide expectation for administrators to set is to ensure teachers display a visual of each essential learning target—perhaps on thermometers that show the overall percentage of students in the class who are proficient on each essential learning target, as shown in figure 3.5 (page 52). As teams assess each essential learning target, they display the percent proficient, with dates and contrasting colors showing when each additional intervention is complete to show the growth in proficiency over time.

Teams may also consider posting combined proficiencies on each essential learning target in a prominent area, promoting the idea that in a PLC, within teams, all students are "our students" (DuFour et al., 2024).

Students should also track their own progress on each essential learning target in a notebook that corresponds to the display in the classroom. Requiring a parent signature for this strategy is a way to share student proficiency status with parents. An example of student essential standards tracker appears in figure 3.6 (page 53). Students are much more likely to hit targets if they are aware of the target. Parents who are aware of targets can help encourage their children to hit those targets (DuFour et al., 2024). Students who feel overwhelmed by everything they are supposed to learn may feel relief and be able to focus when they know the essential learning is a reasonable amount of material to learn.

Common Formative Assessment 1	
I can add, subtract, and multiply polynomials. Block 1	I can add, subtract, and multiply polynomials. Block 2
96% 9/8/25 / 16% 8/28/25	67% 9/8/25 / 12% 8/28/25
I can add, subtract, and multiply polynomials. Block 3	I can add, subtract, and multiply polynomials. Block 5
62% 9/8/25 / 0% 8/28/25	76% 9/8/25 / 4% 8/28/25
I can add, subtract, and multiply polynomials. Block 6	I can add, subtract, and multiply polynomials. Block 8
90% 9/8/25 / 50% 8/28/25	60% 9/8/25 / 48% 8/28/25

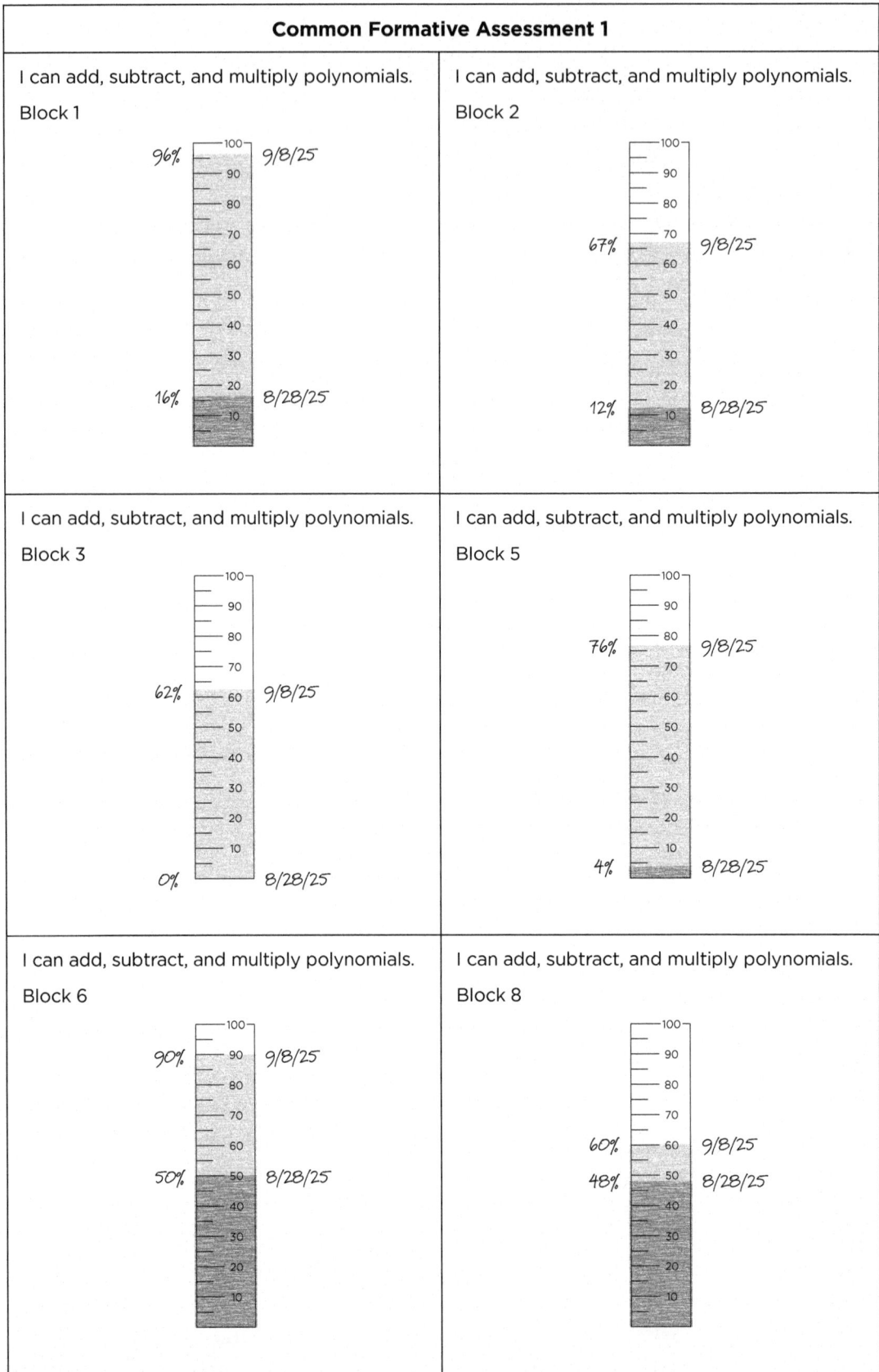

FIGURE 3.5: Visual of student progress on an essential learning target posted on a classroom wall.

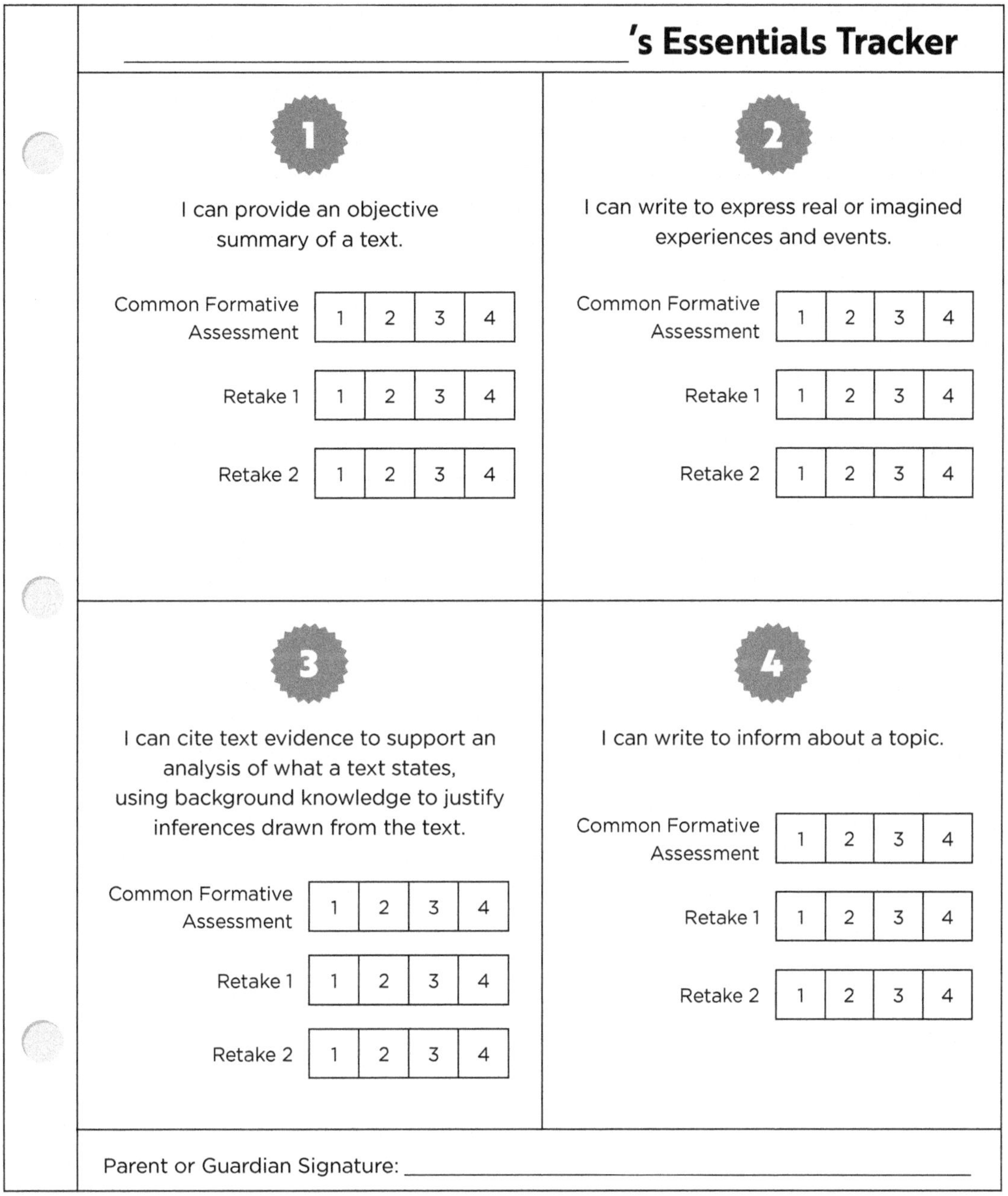

______________________'s Essentials Tracker

1 I can provide an objective summary of a text.

Common Formative Assessment	1	2	3	4
Retake 1	1	2	3	4
Retake 2	1	2	3	4

2 I can write to express real or imagined experiences and events.

Common Formative Assessment	1	2	3	4
Retake 1	1	2	3	4
Retake 2	1	2	3	4

3 I can cite text evidence to support an analysis of what a text states, using background knowledge to justify inferences drawn from the text.

Common Formative Assessment	1	2	3	4
Retake 1	1	2	3	4
Retake 2	1	2	3	4

4 I can write to inform about a topic.

Common Formative Assessment	1	2	3	4
Retake 1	1	2	3	4
Retake 2	1	2	3	4

Parent or Guardian Signature: ______________________

Source: Hot Springs Junior Academy, Arkansas. Used with permission.

FIGURE 3.6: Student notebook tracking of essential learning targets (first page only).

Visit ***go.SolutionTree.com/PLCbooks*** *to download a free reproducible version of this figure.*

Students could also use their notebooks showing proficiency on the essential learning targets to lead parent conferences, where students would be able to indicate their own strengths and areas for improvement. Secondary teachers could consider identifying the essential learning targets in their electronic gradebook so that parents can clearly see whether their child has demonstrated proficiency or not.

It is important that every student knows why the essential learning targets matter, what proficiency looks like, and when they have reached it. In secondary classrooms, students should be able to tell class by class if they have met the essential learning targets. Teams can use a visual in the hallway for all the students to see; this information is also reflected in the Team and Singleton tab of the PLC Dashboard (see chapter 5, page 107).

It might take some trial and error for teams to determine which systems of tracking and displays work best, but just like in video games, targets must be clear and feedback must be quick. In the meantime, teachers should now be ready to move forward with step 2 of the seven-step learning cycle.

TEACHERS TALK

"As a new teacher, the discussion that took place when my team was determining an essential learning target really helped me to know how to spend my time instructing." —Berni D.

"This work helped us get to the heart of a unit, as coverage of all seemed so undoable. This helped sharpen our focus to what mattered most." —Mark S.

STEP 1: DETERMINE THE ESSENTIAL LEARNING TARGET

PAUSE AND REFLECT

In what ways do you think this step would impact the students you serve?

Evidence you are getting it right:

- Teams and singletons know and have prioritized their standards.
- Teams have used the R.E.A.L. criteria to deem standards essential.
- Essential learning targets come from the standards.
- Teams and singletons know what students need for success when they enter the next grade level.
- Teams can come to consensus on essential learning targets.
- Teams and singletons are excited to see the evidence of how students will do on each essential learning target.
- Students, parents, special education providers, English learning teachers, and other teachers are aware of the team- and singleton-determined essential learning targets.
- Every student at the grade level will be taught, and is expected to learn, each essential learning target.
- Teams have made plans to communicate the results of essential learning targets to students and parents.

Evidence you aren't there yet:

- The team or singleton decides to just use the essentials standards identified by the district.
- The job of determining essential learning targets is assigned to a committee on campus.
- Teams can't decide on the essential learning targets.
- The team or singleton determines that everything is essential.
- A singleton teacher decides not to participate in this step because they don't have a team.

What is a strength from this step that may already be going well on campus that you could acknowledge and celebrate?

Step 2: Set a SMART Goal and Create the Common Formative Assessment

This step comes before the team or singleton has begun teaching and has two parts: (1) Determining SMART goals for student proficiency on the essential learning target and (2) creating the common formative assessment.

Determining SMART Goals

If someone were planning to run a marathon, it would be reasonable to set a goal for the time expected to complete the run. While some might say their goal is to just finish the race, those looking to improve over time would set a time-bound goal, such as finishing the marathon in under four hours. This overall goal helps sharpen focus, yet those who want to be most prepared for the race would also need some short-term goals to help them reach the overall goal.

These short-term SMART goals are exactly what effective teams and singletons need to set once they have determined the essential learning target for the unit. While the hope is to get 100 percent of the students to proficiency regardless of which teacher they are assigned to, and regardless of the groups students might be part of (English language learners, students with 504s, students with IEPs, and so on), it takes time and a lot of team learning to build up to that level. When teachers work in the ongoing seven-step learning cycle, setting incrementally increasing SMART goals will help them get closer and closer to the most important of the three big ideas of a PLC, learning for all (DuFour et al., 2024). In the second (implementing) stage of the PLC Dashboard, teams and singletons will track their SMART-goal attainment, indicating if the teachers are getting the expected results.

To work up to 100 percent learning for all, effective teams and singletons set SMART goals. SMART goals are (Conzemius & O'Neill, 2013):

- Specific and strategic
- Measurable

- Attainable
- Results-oriented
- Time bound

Effective SMART goals focus teams on both the expected results and the timetable to which they are committing to get those results. Noted business author Patrick Lencioni (2012) states, "Even well-intentioned members of a team need to be held accountable if a team is going to stick to its decisions and accomplish its goals" (p. 54). Lencioni (2012) goes on to state that "peer-to-peer accountability is the primary and most effective source of accountability on the leadership team of a healthy organization" (p. 54). These are some of the reasons that effective collaborative teams set SMART goals.

An effective SMART goal does not need to be complex; it details the percent of all students in a grade level or course who will be proficient on the essential learning target by an upcoming date. For example, 65 percent of first graders will be proficient in counting to 120 by January 14.

Teams set SMART goals before the unit begins and revisit them when the unit (and interventions) are complete to see if they met the goal. Teams, singletons, the guiding coalition, and administrators will recognize when SMART goals are met, since they are a major focus of the PLC Dashboard. The data collected with each cycle of the seven-step learning cycle impacts the SMART goal the next time the team teaches the same essential learning target, getting teams closer to the ultimate SMART goal of 100 percent learning for all students with each cycle of learning. This is the aim of the learning of teams, and by sharing what strategies achieve the best results every time teams work through the seven-step learning cycle, teams are actively working to improve their teaching techniques.

In this step, teams set SMART goals for all students in a course or grade level. This reduces competition among teachers and increases the chance that teachers will work together for the benefit of the students they collectively serve. I do not encourage teachers to share their SMART goals with students. The message to students is that every student must learn the essential learning targets, but behind the scenes, effective teacher teams set SMART goals and look to improve them with each passing year, especially as teachers are learning new skills from colleagues and making changes to their instruction through the process.

To be clear, singletons also set a SMART goal for each essential learning target. They might not be able to create a *common* formative assessment, but they can create a formative assessment.

If a team is going to spend the energy and time determining what is essential for students to learn, it just makes sense to measure whether students have learned it or not. DuFour and colleagues (2024) remind us of this fundamental PLC product by stating, "In high-performing PLCs, the assessment process also must include team-developed common formative assessments" (p. 170). Besides revealing which students have learned the essential learning target and which have not, teacher teams also use common formative assessments to determine which instructional practices are yielding the best results.

Creating the Common Formative Assessment

The entire seven-step learning cycle depends on a team-developed common formative assessment; without a common formative assessment, the rest of the seven-step learning cycle doesn't exist. Teachers should create a common formative assessment at the same time their team makes a SMART goal before teaching the unit. This encourages teachers to begin with the end in mind and link their assessments in their Essential Learning Target Plans. Singletons still need to create formative assessments, but they may be slightly different from the team-created common formative assessment, depending on the on-ramp the singleton is utilizing (see chapter 2, page 23).

Often, when I am working with schools as a consultant, I start really simple. I hand out index cards to teachers asking them to write one thing they think is essential for every student in their class to know or be able to do in the next month of school. Teachers then share what they wrote with their collaborative teams and reach consensus on one essential learning target. Then, each team writes a short common formative assessment to measure that target. This ignites the process in schools, as teachers genuinely want to know if the students can or cannot do the essential learning target they are going to assess.

That hunger for data is maximized when teachers are the ones deciding what to assess and how to assess it, which is why the common formative assessment must be team created. If you are a principal or instructional coach, you may have great ideas for this and want to influence what your teachers pick as essential. I encourage you to see your role here as a coach to guide them to choose what they want based on the R.E.A.L. criteria from the first step. Teachers will experience growth in the process of choosing over time as results will vary. Trusting collaborative teams and singletons and letting them learn from occasional bad choices are important parts of this learning process.

While teams can sometimes easily reach agreement on what is essential, writing the common formative assessment can really challenge a team, as the rigor expected of students is determined at this step. One science team experienced this when they selected knowledge of the scientific method as their essential learning target in a unit. The common formative assessment they settled on required very little rigor by only asking students to select the correct order of the scientific method from four options. While a very informal preassessment had shown that almost none of the students were even familiar with the scientific method, after one or two lessons, the common assessment revealed almost a 100 percent passing rate across the school. At that point, there was no learning available for the teachers to glean from one another, and student evidence of success on the common formative assessment did not necessarily indicate that the student would be proficient in the overall subject. By completing the cycle and reviewing the data, the teachers knew the rigor wasn't adequate, but they had to learn it for themselves.

Think of the common formative assessment like a quiz rather than like an end-of-chapter test. It can be as short as one question with several versions to reduce cheating or to avoid having students simply memorize the answers. The common formative assessment could also be a performance assessment, such as a speech or a project. One key is that the common formative assessment is at a rigor level similar to the overall standard and that when graded, it will easily allow the teacher to put students into two distinct groups: those who are proficient and those who are not proficient yet, based on the success criteria the team established. According to Paul Bambrick-Santoyo (2019), "Standards are meaningless until you define how to assess them" (p. 21). This is a reminder that it is the rigor of the assessment, not the standards by themselves that matters most. In addition, sticking to one essential learning target on each common formative assessment at first can help collaborative teams determine intervention grouping much easier, as adding more learning targets on an assessment makes it harder for a teacher to determine those two groups. As teams grow in the process, they can add additional essential learning targets to common formative assessments over time.

Another key is that common formative assessments have actionable data. Kim Bailey and Chris Jakicic (2017) emphasize that for educators to diagnose specific student needs, assessment questions must be based on learning targets rather than standards. This targeted information gives teams insights to diagnose and respond with additional time and support for their students.

During the creation of common formative assessments, educators should do the following.

1. Consider the depth of knowledge (DOK) level of the standard at the grade level and match the rigor of the common formative assessment to it.

2. Ensure that a student showing proficiency on the common formative assessment would be a good indicator that the student would also be proficient on other indicators of achievement, such as an interim or end-of-year assessment.

3. Check to see that individual student common formative assessment results could allow educators to quickly and easily put students in either an intervention or an extension and would know what skill to target.

Figures 3.7 and 3.8 are two team-created common formative assessments that quickly inform educators which students are proficient in the concept and which students need more support.

Name: _____ Date: _____

Writing standard: I can write arguments to support claims with clear reasons and relevant evidence.

> Solar power is a great benefit to humanity, but it also comes with some disadvantages. Solar power is infinitely renewable, can significantly decrease monthly energy bills, can allow homes and cities to become energy independent, and is beneficial to the environment. Two downsides to solar power are the large upfront costs of installation and the inability to generate power when clouds are present, which happens more in some areas than others. Sometimes these upfront costs can be offset by government subsidies, but the community is still paying the costs, regardless of the funding source.

Write your own claim based on the paragraph above and support it with evidence from the text.

_____

_____

_____

_____

FIGURE 3.7: Sample grade 7 team-created common formative assessment.

Ann has 7 blocks. 5 blocks are red. The others are blue. How many blocks are blue?

5 red	? blue
7 blocks	

_____ **blue blocks**

FIGURE 3.8: Sample grade 1 team-created common formative assessment.

SMART goals go hand in hand with the common formative assessment since the common formative assessment assesses whether the goal has been reached. Here is how the two would work together: A collaborative team could set a goal for an essential learning target in a unit of study based on the percentage of students (or specific number of students) who will be proficient. (For example: By October 10, 75 percent of grade 6 students will be able to support a claim with clear reasons and relevant evidence proficiently.) In this example, the collaborative team will give the common formative assessment of this essential learning target several days prior to October 10; then, after sharing and discussing the results, it will regroup students for short-duration reteaching and intervention and extension for the remaining days prior to the end of the unit on October 10. The team must set aside time before October 10 to give a different version of the same common formative assessment to those students who were in the intervention group. The steps of discussing and comparing results and intervening and extending with students are discussed further in steps 5 and 6 (pages 65 and 72).

There is a danger that if teams believe they absolutely must meet the SMART goal, they will either (1) lower the rigor on the common formative assessment, or (2) lower the SMART goal so that it can easily be achieved. Administrators and teachers must resist these temptations. It is much more beneficial for teams to have challenging goals and rigorous common formative assessments that don't meet those goals than it is to have teams that meet goals while the student results on other measures, such as end-of-year testing, just aren't improving. One way to avoid this danger is for a guiding coalition or a principal to celebrate a team whose common formative assessment data starts at, say, 37 percent proficient and then through intervention goes up to 51 percent proficient, and then to 57 percent after yet another intervention cycle, even if the SMART goal is 75 percent proficiency. When administrators and teams celebrate progress and growth like this, it reinforces to everyone that *true student growth results are valued over SMART goal attainment.*

Experienced teams will have made many decisions together at this stage.

- They defined the success criteria students must meet. Students above that proficiency level on the common formative assessment will receive an extension, and students below will receive intervention.

- They created alternate versions of the common formative assessment to reduce cheating.

- They determined how to communicate with students and parents which students have and have not learned the essential learning target.

At this point, teams have created the SMART goal and the common formative assessment, taught the material for the first time, and are ready to give the common formative assessment for the first time.

TEACHERS TALK

"Giving common formative assessments on the same day became a really critical part to our unit planning process, and kept all of us together. At times it did feel restrictive, but we needed it." —Mark S.

STEP 2: SET A SMART GOAL AND CREATE THE COMMON FORMATIVE ASSESSMENT

PAUSE AND REFLECT

In what ways do you think this step would impact the students you serve?

Evidence you are getting it right:

- Teachers have a goal that is not too easy and will stretch the team.
- Teachers use prior year SMART goals as a baseline for improvement each year to get closer to learning for all.
- Teachers use calendars to plan out dates for units of study, common formative assessments, inter-rater reliability, and interventions and extensions, as well as dates to meet to reflect and see if they met the goals they set.
- Teachers use rubrics, exemplars, or other methods to describe success.
- Everyone on the team knows what the assessment looks like and the success criteria of each assessment.

Evidence you aren't there yet:

- The team does not set a goal for student achievement on essential learning targets, for any reason, and they don't have a baseline with which to start.
- The team does not know the goal that was set.
- The team shares the SMART goal with students, instead of telling students, "All of you must learn this important concept."
- A unit begins, and the teachers do not know what the assessment is that will measure proficiency on the essential learning target.

What is a strength from this step to acknowledge and celebrate?

Step 3: Give the Common Formative Assessment

This is an exciting time; teachers should be eager to know if students have learned what they taught. Author Mike Schmoker (2006) reminds educators of the many benefits of formative assessment when he states, "Formative assessments not only inform productive adjustments to instruction but also ensure consistently delivered, viable curriculum as they allow teams to see, on a frequent basis, that their efforts are paying off" (p. 123).

Prior to giving students the assessment, teachers must discuss the conditions for giving the assessment, including determining whether they will allow notes, the level of assistance teachers can give, the anchor charts that students can see, the time allowed for the assessment, and any other variables that could impact results. This may include any preassessment reviews that teachers will conduct and any resources students will be allowed to use during the assessment. Teams must come to agreement on these assessment conditions.

Team members must also administer the common formative assessment on the same day. While the goal is to accomplish this, if a teacher is absent or dates must be adjusted due to unforeseen events, there can be exceptions. Teams should not allow the common formative assessment date to be fluid as a rule, however, especially if one teacher on the team simply states that their students are not ready. If one teacher is ready to give the common formative assessment and another teacher is not, delaying the common formative assessment would mean the ready teacher would have to scramble to alter their plans. This does not build good team chemistry. If the ready teacher still gives the common formative assessment, but the teacher that isn't ready does not for a few days, the ready teacher might conclude that if their students had three more days, they would have gotten better results, too. Put simply, common formative assessments need to be given on the same day across a team for the cycle to move forward in a meaningful and systematic way that is equitable to students. Teachers who give assessments on a schedule are much more likely to get through the guaranteed and viable curriculum—a key to student academic achievement.

It is also important to remember that one of the main purposes of the seven-step learning cycle is for teachers to learn from one another. If one teacher didn't think their students were ready for the common formative assessment, but another teacher's students were ready, the not-ready teacher could likely learn what the ready teacher did to prepare the students. For multiple purposes in the process, the constraint of giving common formative assessments on the same day is intentional.

Once they have given the common formative assessment, the team is ready to determine how they will align grading practices to ensure each teacher sees student proficiency the same way. This is the next step.

STEP 3: GIVE THE COMMON FORMATIVE ASSESSMENT

PAUSE AND REFLECT

In what ways do you think this step would impact the students you serve?

Evidence you are getting it right:

- A student who is successful on this common formative assessment would be highly correlated to a student who is successful on larger measures of student academic achievement.

- There are a few versions of the assessment to reduce cheating.

- Teachers on the same team administer common formative assessments on the same day, and they assist students in similar ways across classrooms.

- The students who are unsuccessful on the common formative assessment will be easy to group by skill for intervention.

- The team is eager to get the common formative assessment results back.

Evidence you aren't there yet:

- Teachers do not have a plan for what day they will give the common formative assessment before the teaching starts.

- Teachers routinely do not give common formative assessments on the same day.

- Teachers do not give the same common formative assessment.

- Some students can just memorize the answers on the common formative assessment, as there are no alternate versions of it.

What is a strength from this step to acknowledge and celebrate?

Step 4: Ensure Inter-Rater Reliability

This step is about ensuring inter-rater reliability and is also known as *calibrating* or *co-grading*. According to the Rhode Island Department of Education (RIDE; n.d.):

> The purpose of calibration is to ensure that a group of educators evaluates student work consistently and in alignment with the scoring rubric. This increases the reliability of the assessment data . . . and deepens educators' understanding of expectations for student work.

A critical component of the seven-step cycle is for teachers to be able to share their results with their teammates and know that they truly have an "apples to apples" comparison. For a comparison of results to have useful application to student interventions or to determine which instructional practices had the greatest impact, teachers must establish inter-rater reliability, the practice of ensuring that multiple teachers grade student proficiency the same way, prior to grading student assessments. Ensuring strong inter-rater reliability puts a team at DuFour and colleagues' (2024) highest level on a key continuum for monitoring student learning. In addition, according to Douglas Reeves (2000), author of a landmark study focusing on the academic achievement of over 130,000 high-poverty students where more than 90 percent achieved proficiency:

> While many schools continue to rely upon the idiosyncratic judgment of individual teachers for a definition of "proficiency," the high-achieving schools made it clear that no accident of geography or classroom assignment would determine expectations for students. (p. 191)

This study related the importance of ensuring all certified educators at a school are involved in establishing inter-rater reliability of student work, particularly in writing. Consider an art or social studies teacher who would like to incorporate some writing into their curriculum. If they know the grade-level expectations for writing of the English language arts department, they would be more likely to uphold those expectations, which could have a significant effect on the rigor levels that eventually all teachers throughout a school contribute to upholding.

After a team has given the assessments, one way of ensuring inter-rater reliability is for teachers to gather several random, ungraded assessments. Some teams have norms that they meet during a planning period or at lunch after even just one class has taken the assessment. Some teams meet after school on the day the assessment was given to ensure this is done. Regardless of how the team wants to ensure this critical step occurs, the date of establishing inter-rater reliability should be planned.

When teams meet for this purpose, members put one ungraded assessment on a screen using a document camera or make a copy of an assessment, so each team member is looking at the same assessment. Then each member can individually grade the assessment alone prior to any discussion. When all members of the team have graded the assessment, members share their results and rationale for grading. Teams repeat this process with three or four student assessments, at which point teams are usually aligned enough so that a proficient assessment graded by one teacher would also be graded a proficient assessment by the others. An alternative is for each member of the team to have a different and ungraded student assessment. Each teacher grades the assessment they have by writing the grade on a sticky note and placing it on the back of the assessment. Members then pass the assessment along to the next person who grades it on a sticky note. When the assessments have made it all the way around the team, team members compare and discuss the grades to establish inter-rater reliability. High variability in grades of the same assessment warrants more discussion among team members and will possibly lead to alterations of the rubric.

It is important that when team members work to establish inter-rater reliability, they do not reveal any qualifying statements about the student work they are grading. For instance, if a teacher says, "The student we will grade next is one of my honors students," that information may bias the grades that the other teachers give. Teams should simply share the unnamed student work to be graded without comment. This helps to increase objectivity and lets everyone look at students' work on its own merits.

Ensuring inter-rater reliability is intended to inform and improve teacher practice and bring clarity to what proficiency looks like. In addition, when this step is done well, teachers are better equipped to communicate the success criteria to their own students, "who can then assess the quality of their own work and become more actively engaged in their learning" (DuFour et al., 2024, p. 187).

Once this process is completed, teachers can then grade their students' assessments. More advanced teams might trade all their assessments at this point and grade the assessments of their teammates' students. This increases accountability to return assessments to students more quickly so they get feedback sooner, and it reduces subjectivity that teachers can have about their students, such as, "Jesse knows this—he just didn't write it—so I'm going to give him the credit." It also increases the team's feeling of ownership of all students in that grade level or subject.

Importantly, if teachers do not take the time to ensure they grade proficiency similarly, there is no value in sharing common formative assessment results (step 5 in the cycle) to discover the most effective instructional practices. Without ensuring inter-rater reliability, intervention and extension grouping is also arbitrary; by doing the work to ensure a common understanding of proficiency, however, students get the intervention and extension they need, regardless of the teacher to whom they were assigned.

Another benefit of the equity that ensuring inter-rater reliability provides comes when teachers get questions and push back from parents and students in response to student grades. It is extremely helpful when teachers receive this feedback to be able to inform parents and students of how the team established the proficiency criteria together and practiced with several assessments to ensure they would grade student proficiency equitably. This step allows teachers to have clarity on what the team expects students to be able to do so teachers are better able to hold higher standards with students.

Teams repeat the process for ensuring inter-rater reliability for every common formative assessment they give. Teams should do their best to stick to the dates for this step. For singletons working in isolation, this is the only step in the seven-step cycle that is eliminated since there is only one teacher who will be grading student work.

TEACHERS TALK

"Establishing inter-rater reliability was the most important piece to our team to truly see what other kids were capable of. It helped me to know that I could push my kids to that level. When I saw their great work in other classes, I said, 'This is what my students should be able to do!'" —Brandi S.

"This step helped my team define what rigor looked like, and the inter-rater reliability held me and my colleagues to that rigor." —Liz H.

STEP 4: ENSURE INTER-RATER RELIABILITY

PAUSE AND REFLECT

In what ways do you think this step would impact the students you serve?

Evidence you are getting it right:

- A proficient score in one classroom would be a proficient score in any other classroom.

- Teams further refine success criteria so that clarity of expectations for students continues to grow.

- Teams are willing to and often grade the assessments of students who are not in their own classrooms.

Evidence you aren't there yet:

- Each teacher has a different standard of proficiency on common formative assessments.

- All assessments are multiple choice, so there is no need for establishing inter-rater reliability. (Note: It is better to have a balance of assessment types—some multiple choice, some constructed response, and some performance items and tasks.)

- Inter-rater reliability is done after teachers have graded the common formative assessments.

- This step is done many days after teachers have given common formative assessments, which further delays the feedback to students.

- This step is skipped.

What is a strength from this step to acknowledge and celebrate?

Step 5: Share Results

Each member of a collaborative team must be able to determine which students have met proficiency and which students have not based on the team's criteria, and all team members must collect and organize their data in a similar manner. Some teams might use a column in the gradebook or a spreadsheet that tracks student proficiency of the essential learning targets skill by skill, and student by student. Regardless of the format teams use, the way teams organize results must facilitate their ability to compare results to determine which instructional strategies are getting the best results. Karin Chenoweth (2017), former reporter and the author of *It's Being Done: Academic Success in Unexpected Schools* states:

> The most powerful conversation that can occur in any school is when one teacher says to another, "Your kids did better than mine. What did you do?"

And that conversation can happen only when teachers are looking at data from the same assessments of the same subject matter given at roughly the same time. (p. 199)

In PLCs, educators learn by looking through the lens of common formative assessments. The results help teachers determine intervention and extension grouping, form the basis of the discussions teachers have about how to improve their instruction, and let administrators know what instructional strategies to showcase to other staff members based on which strategies proved most effective. Eventually, teams and singletons record student proficiency results in the PLC Dashboard so that every educator on campus can quickly see the status of student learning in the school.

I recommend teams determine the format they will use to collect student common formative assessment results prior to recording the data in the PLC Dashboard to increase the likelihood of fidelity. I once worked with a team that did not determine the format, and one team member came to the meeting where results would be discussed with his student proficiency percentage written on a torn-off piece of paper. It said "100%." The other teammates brought spreadsheets showing essential learning target proficiency for each student, and their results were much less stellar. As you can imagine, there was widespread disbelief that one teacher's 100 percent proficiency was an accurate representation of the facts, and thus the rest of the cycle could not be completed with fidelity.

Consider the team of three grade 7 mathematics teachers. Notice in figure 3.9 how the three grade 7 teachers have a similar way to collect student results and can easily tell which teacher is getting the best results.

CFA 1 Results by Class Period and Teacher	
Christensen Period 1	63% proficient
Christensen Period 5	58% proficient
Christensen Total	60% proficient
Kennedy Period 3	44% proficient
Kennedy Period 6	52% proficient
Kennedy Period 7	38% proficient
Kennedy Total	46% proficient
Meyer Period 2	89% proficient
Meyer Period 5	78% proficient
Meyer Total	84% proficient

FIGURE 3.9: Sample sharing of overall student results.

Some believe this step in the cycle is uncomfortable for adults. That may very well be true in the beginning, but vulnerability with results on an agreed-upon essential learning target among teams promotes best practices and results for the students we serve. Teacher comfort is important, but the most important people in the learning process are the students. If a teacher team is not willing or able to share results, principals must ensure the team has the support, encouragement, gentle and consistent accountability, and, occasionally, the enforcement they need to ensure this critical process is completed.

Ensure teachers understand that sharing results is not done to judge one another, but rather to help the team determine which teaching methods achieve the best results. Sometimes the best strategies get results for certain groups of students, but not others (English learners or students with dyslexia, for example). In this case, teams evaluate the results with a focus on what is working best for specific groups and add those teaching techniques to their teacher toolbox.

On the same spreadsheet teams use to keep track of student proficiency on each essential learning target, they also track student proficiency on the most recent end-of-year state assessment as well as the most recent interim assessment, as shown in figure 3.10 (page 68). This spreadsheet is hyperlinked as part of the PLC Dashboard, as discussed in chapter 5 (page 107).

For the first essential learning targets of the school year, this might be the score the student earned on the end-of-year results from the previous school year. This allows teams to do a quick check as they enter student results to see if there is any correlation between the larger assessments and the common formative assessment, which is ideal. Simply put, correlation would be when students who score low on an end-of-year assessment also score low on a common formative assessment, and students who score high on end-of-year assessments also score high on common formative assessments. Annually, you should determine which common formative assessments are most correlated with larger assessments and which are not. Teams should examine those common formative assessments that are least correlated to determine if they need to adjust the rigor of the common formative assessment or if they need to select a different essential learning target.

Often, teams will not have similarly heterogenous groups of students (a roughly equal blend of students who are higher and lower performing) and therefore results will be skewed when sharing. While organizing students based on ability levels should be done sparingly (Marzano, 2019; Marzano et al., 2001), sometimes classes have a high concentration of students with greater needs based on constraints within the master schedule. When this happens, I encourage teams to compare proficiency of similar student groups, such as English learners, from one teacher to another. Teams can also select a common group of students to compare prior to teaching the unit, even if that means omitting some student data. This is done only to find the most effective instructional techniques among similar groups of students and wouldn't impact the need for students below proficient to receive intervention.

Even if results are roughly the same for teachers across the team, instructional techniques among those teachers can vary widely. These are opportunities for teams to allow each teacher to share their strategies to improve each teacher's instructional repertoire, and for teachers to use those strategies to reach even more students.

When results are low across a team, teams need to seek outside help from the district, from additional research, or from consultation with administration, and study as a group how to improve results.

TEACHERS TALK

"This results spreadsheet really zeros in on whether students are 'getting it' or not. The running tally that shows growth over time emphasizes the process, that students don't learn rigorous things overnight." —Mark S.

"It was great to track results to see what really worked and what didn't. It made me ask more questions about my practices." —Scott S.

Class Period	Student	ACT Reading Spring 2025	MAP Reading Fall 2025	MAP Reading Winter 2025	MAP Reading Spring 2026	CFA 1	Retake	Retake	CFA 2	Retake	Retake	CFA 3	Retake	Retake
3	Jason Z.	390	214	211	216	40	50	80	40	60	80	40	54	70
3	Myles B.	420	235	239	239	93			92			80	85	
3	Ashley M.	400	220	222	224	63	74	82	74	100		90	90	
3	Saira T.	433	237	240	234	90			75	92		74	90	
3	Oliver K.	392	201	209	216	50	74	70	60	92		56	68	76
3	Jamarcus R.	433	229	233	240	80	80		71	71	80	100		
3	Kam F.	432	2323	249	245	100			100			100		
3	Andrew R.	410	222	229	223	77	90		74	88		72	90	
3	Norah E.	380	200	204	212	40	60	80	10	68	72	70	80	
3	Quan H.	430	234	230	230	77	77		63	83	90	90	90	
3	Danesh S.	388	216	226	231	58	90		67	83		70	70	80
3	Mia B.	416	220	210	218	93	95		92	92		56	72	84
3	Jorge R.	402	220	220	226	83	100		88			80	100	

For the first four score columns, ■ red, ■ yellow, ■ green, and ■ blue represent increasing levels of proficiency. In the CFA columns, ■ red is below proficient and ■ green is above.

FIGURE 3.10: Sample student results spreadsheet.

STEP 5: SHARE RESULTS

PAUSE AND REFLECT

In what ways do you think this step would impact the students you serve?

Evidence you are getting it right:

- The time between giving the common formative assessment, ensuring inter-rater reliability, and sharing results is measured in days, not weeks.
- The team knows that this process is not about judging one another but about getting better at the challenging task of student learning.
- Poor results by one or more team members are seen as a learning opportunity for the whole team.
- Teachers examine results from groups of students (such as English learners, students with IEPs, gifted students, and so on) to see if any techniques proved especially effective for them.

Evidence you aren't there yet:

- Members of a team do not know, skill by skill and student by student, who has and who has not demonstrated proficiency on common formative assessments.
- Teams share individual teacher results outside of the team as gossip.
- It is difficult to know which students are below proficiency and which are at or above proficiency.

What is a strength from this step to acknowledge and celebrate?

Step 6: Develop and Carry Out an Action Plan for Intervention and Extension

Developing an action plan focuses teams and singletons on defining exactly what the educators will do with those students who have and have not learned essential learning targets. As DuFour and colleagues (2024) note, when there is not a systematic response from a team to ensure students receive additional learning opportunities when results indicate they have not learned, this reduces assessments students have taken to tests administered solely to assign a grade.

It is during this step that teams will make their plans for intervention and extension. This task can be broken up among team members so some plan intervention while others plan extension. The actual intervention and extension can include set times when teachers on the team trade students so that those who require the same intervention or extension are together. Teachers can also differentiate within a class for the intervention and extension time, with each teacher using the team's plans with both groups during the in-class time. Regardless of how teams break up responsibilities, they should record their specific reteaching plans, including dates and times.

Students then retake the common formative assessment at the conclusion of the team-determined interventions, often with a different version of the same assessment to reduce the possibility of students memorizing the answers. An alternative is for students to demonstrate their proficiency on an end-of-unit assessment where the essential learning target might be a small part of the overall assessment. Regardless of how students are reassessed, teams need to know if the interventions achieved the intended results.

While teams are developing their action plan, it is also a great time for them to gather their observations about which instructional strategies are getting the best results from first instruction. This becomes the main driver of professional development for the adults, especially for those educators on the team with higher percentages of students who did not at first attain proficiency.

While finalizing the action plan should take place on the date the team determined to share their results, initial planning should not wait until this date as that can delay the implementation of the action plan. Effective teams begin their general planning for intervention and extension well before they know exactly which students will need more support and before teams learn which teachers achieved the best results or student growth. This enables teacher teams to provide feedback and intervention more rapidly to students, both of which produce positive impacts on student learning (Hattie, 2023).

Some keys for intervention planning in class include the following.

- Ensure that intervention is not seen as punishment. Some schools call it WIN time—What I Need time.
- Utilize the instructional techniques that got the best initial results for the students who need it the most.
- Discover from colleagues different ways to teach the same essential learning targets.
- Utilize (occasionally) effective volunteer peer tutors during interventions.
- Schedule the intervention ahead of time.
- Consider using different teaching modalities for the intervention (visual, auditory, or kinesthetic).
- Be specific about dates, times, and activities the essential learning target intervention is addressing.

Some keys for extension planning in class include the following.

- Ensure that extension is not seen as a reward but instead is part of the learning process.
- Give students several choices for their extension activity.
- Limit the number of questions students in the extension group can ask the teacher so the teacher can focus mostly on the intervention group. This also encourages the extension group to work together.

- Plan the extension (and intervention) time with team members so that individual teachers don't have to do all the planning themselves.
- Select nice-to-know (not essential to know) material as extensions.

Occasionally, I encounter schools that do not schedule some students to be a part of the Tier 1 instruction at grade level. This usually occurs with students who have an IEP and with English learners. All students who will eventually be independently functioning adults must have access to highly effective instruction of the essential learning targets for their grade level if we expect those students to catch up and keep up.

Students who still haven't learned the essential learning target after the in-class interventions when the unit ends would be ready for Tier 2 intervention. Tier 2 includes the interventions that take place for students who need additional support after a unit of study is complete. The interventions, which some call "in-class reteaching," listed in step 6 of the seven-step learning cycle, are at Tier 1. These occur before the unit ends and mostly in class during regular class time soon after the common formative assessment. After in-class interventions, students still below proficiency should be re-assessed on another version of the team-created common formative assessment. Alternatively, teams can also check student proficiency during an end-of-unit assessment that measures the essential learning target. Keep in mind, however, that no amount of intervention can overcome ineffective teaching, and therefore it is critical that teachers capture team learning in step 7 of the seven-step learning cycle and grow as professionals as a result of working through the cycle with each essential learning target.

Principals who recognize ineffective teaching techniques should work on implementing more effective techniques across the campus, or at least in the pockets where ineffective techniques exist. In many schools where incoming student achievement is low, it will take time to boost proficiency; educators in those schools should not lose hope but instead stay focused and not get discouraged, as proficiency will improve over time while professionals are learning with one another.

Often, two or three sessions of intervention during class, spread out over a few days in roughly twenty-minute increments or whatever fits the master schedule, is appropriate for this step. The goal of this step is to get to the proficiency percentages established in the team-determined SMART goal (or higher) by the time interventions at this step are complete. That goal will vary widely in the beginning as teams are learning the process.

If interventions and extensions are left up to individual teacher discretion, some students will receive additional time and support, and some won't. When teams do not determine their action plans together, significant inequities result.

TEACHERS TALK

"The mindset that every student will learn our essentials was critical. It really lit a fire under us as a team to ensure student learning, even if it took some students more time to get there." —Mindy W.

PAUSE AND REFLECT

In what ways do you think this step would impact the students you serve?

Evidence you are getting it right:

- Teams and singletons can rapidly identify students by name and by need for support with essential learning targets.

- The intervention is similar regardless of which teacher a student is assigned to.

- The intervention and extension plans are specific to an essential learning target and include dates and specific activities.

- Teams see unsuccessful students as our students who need more support.

- The team has developed a plan for students who are already proficient that will extend their learning.

- The plans include methods to ensure students have clear, specific, and timely feedback.

Evidence you aren't there yet:

- What happens to a struggling student mostly depends on what the student's teacher decides to do about it, not what the team has decided to do for our students.

- Time is not set aside for intervention and extension for many reasons, such as there is too much curriculum to cover and there isn't time.

- The whole class is a part of the intervention, even when there are some students in the class who demonstrated proficiency on the common formative assessment.

- The intervention or extensions are generic.

- Extensions are an afterthought or non-existent.

What is a strength from this step to acknowledge and celebrate?

Step 7: Capture Team Learning and Make Changes to Instruction

Step 7 gets to the heart of the PLC process. It is about capturing both what to do next for students who haven't learned the essential curriculum as well as which methods of teaching and intervention were the most effective. This step directly helps teachers grow in their skills, and, as Schmoker (2006) reminds us, "teachers learn best from one another" (p. 120). Those teachers with lower student scores on assessments should be expected to learn from those with higher student scores and adjust their teaching methods to try to increase their results as well.

However, sometimes it is difficult to get teachers to change ineffective teaching practices. DuFour (2015) addresses this when he states, "Among the most powerful motivators for persuading educators to change their practice are (1) concrete evidence of irrefutably better results and (2) the positive peer pressure inherent in being a member of a collaborative team" (p. 179). When teams set SMART goals in step 2 prior to teaching an essential learning target and share results after common formative assessments in step 5, schools are taking powerful steps to reduce ineffective teaching practices.

I speak often about how rare it is in education for non-PLC school teachers to use data from their colleagues to impact what happens in classrooms. However, that goal should be explicit by ensuring teachers keep a record of changes they have made to their instruction based on common formative assessment data comparison results. As Laura Lipton and Bruce Wellman (2001) assert in their book, *Mentoring Matters*, "Both the mentor and the protégé consistently initiate learning-focused conversations regarding teacher and student learning" (p. 100). This conversation represents the key purpose of adult learning in a PLC.

Consider a simple example involving math teachers who were comparing student results from a common formative assessment about how to add and subtract different signed numbers (such as –4 + 7). The teacher with the best results had a paper ruler taped to each student desk allowing students the ability to move their fingers on the ruler to help them solve the problem. Rulers are now taped to every other math teacher's students' desks, since the teachers observed better results for some students by looking critically at each other's results.

Another example is from an outstanding social studies teacher with many years of experience. The percentage of her students scoring proficient on a rigorous common formative assessment was in the single digits. One of her teammates, a first-year teacher, had results near 50 percent proficient on the same assessment. The seasoned teacher found out that her teammate had much higher expectations for short-constructed responses on all the written activities, including daily warmups, leading up to the common formative assessment, which made the students much more prepared for the grade-level standard rigor on the assessment. The experienced teacher used this information as an opportunity to grow professionally, learned several valuable teaching skills from that partner, and is an even more effective teacher now.

One of the main goals of the seven-step learning cycle is to eliminate ineffective teaching practices. By capturing team learning and documenting any changes to instruction that team members should make, teams grow over time. This documentation creates a record of the most effective initial instructional practices and illuminates other instructional practices used by members of the collaborative team that were not as effective. This data exemplifies Robert Eaker's (2020) sentiment, "The essential question is this: when we teach this unit in the future, how could it be improved?" (p. 64).

There are many ways teams learn through the seven-step learning cycle. Their critical discussions lead to the collection of information about what is working for students and allows teams to separate fact from opinion. Teams capture changes in instruction at two specific points in the cycle: (1) after the common formative assessment to see what worked best in initial instruction, and (2) after carrying out the intervention plan to see which intervention strategies worked best.

If teachers on teams are not routinely making changes to their instruction, based on common formative assessment results or intervention results, alarm bells should be ringing for principals; something is wrong with the seven-step learning cycle as it is being implemented on your campus. Paul Bambrick-Santoyo (2019) puts it simply when he states, "If you don't change your teaching, results will not change" (p. 98).

There are several important discussions for teams to have during this step.

- What intervention strategy got the best results? While the best initial instructional strategy was captured previously, this step captures what worked best for those students who didn't initially learn the essential learning target.

- What common mistakes did students make? Keeping a record of these common mistakes and pointing them out to students can help prevent them from occurring again.

- What additional team learning took place that the team wants to capture? This could include communication with parents that proved effective, YouTube, Khan Academy, or other online videos that helped students, scaffolding, the use of manipulatives, other graphic organizers or sentence starters that aided students, or any other team learning that facilitated student learning.

- What will the team do to intervene with students who still haven't demonstrated their proficiency on this essential learning target? This represents the initial thinking about a Tier 2 intervention plan.

This is also the time to determine if your team has met the SMART goal it set before the unit began. Some teams will have met the goal, and some will not have. Guiding coalitions should celebrate all teams experiencing student growth after each intervention, even when SMART goals aren't met.

Teams should also capture their discussion of the reteaching strategies that worked best for students who didn't initially learn the essential learning target. It could be a link to the specific graphic organizer that made the learning clearer for some students, or a link to a video tutorial that students watched, or specifics about a different teaching modality (such as visual, audio, or kinesthetic methods of learning). The more specifically a team can describe or identify what worked for struggling learners, the more the team will grow in student and teacher learning over time. Teachers can incorporate intervention strategies that worked into lessons that take place before common formative assessments to prevent students from struggling in the future.

Teams should also capture any other team learning they don't want to forget, such as changes to make to the common formative assessment, time needed for a unit, or learning to emphasize the next time they teach a unit. Reflection after acting is a powerful step, and the time teams take to do this is time well spent.

The final step is for documenting the plan for students who still haven't learned the essential learning target, regardless of whether the team has reached its SMART goal or not. While it is rarely possible for teams to reach 100 percent proficiency on each essential learning target, teams didn't call their learning targets "nice to know" targets, but rather "essential" learning targets. Students who still haven't demonstrated proficiency on essential learning targets must be part of the Tier 2 intervention planning that effective schools do in a PLC. The book *Taking Action: A Handbook for RTI at Work, Second Edition* (Mattos et al., 2025) is an excellent resource for schools and teams to use as a step-by-step guide to create a highly effective multitiered system of supports.

The Team and Singleton Information Tab of the PLC Dashboard indicates where student needs are the greatest—which essential learning target has the most students who need Tier 2 support. Chapter 5 (page 107) describes this piece of the PLC Dashboard in detail.

When teams have gone through the seven-step learning cycle with the first essential learning target, celebration is in order. This quick win is important and worthy of acknowledgment. This celebration could be as simple as the guiding coalition or administration acknowledging the team during a staff meeting or giving a quick shout-out to the team in a weekly all-staff email. Once completed, teams are ready to begin the seven-step learning cycle again with the next essential learning target.

STEP 7: CAPTURE TEAM LEARNING AND MAKE CHANGES TO INSTRUCTION

PAUSE AND REFLECT

In what ways do you think this step would impact the students you serve?

Evidence you are getting it right:

- Teams have records of best practices; they know what works for them for each essential learning target.

- Teams use the results of common formative assessments to determine which colleagues' classrooms to observe.

- Teams know which interventions are most effective with which groups of students.

- Teachers get better results each year by working through the seven-step learning cycle in the PLC process.

- Teachers can easily list several instructional strategies that they now use because a colleague got better results on a recent common formative assessment.

- Teachers discontinue strategies that are not getting good student results.

- Teachers use previously successful post-common formative assessment intervention strategies before common formative assessments are given to prevent the need for intervention.

Evidence you aren't there yet:

- Teams have not captured team learning because of time constraints or other reasons.

- Teachers are unable to think of instructional strategies they have learned from a teammate who got better results on a common formative assessment.

- Team reflections are generic and do not represent any specific team learning or changes the team or individuals should make.

What is a strength from this step to acknowledge and celebrate?

NEXT STEPS

Based on what you've learned in this chapter, what two or three next steps will you take to increase teacher clarity on the seven-step process?

Summary

Administrators and teachers must have clarity on how to do the work they are being asked to do in a PLC. The seven-step learning cycle keeps educators focused on the four critical questions of a PLC and includes team and singleton learning as well. Each of the steps in the cycle is captured in the one-page Essential Learning Target Plan, which will be examined next, which becomes the focus of the PLC Dashboard.

Take a moment to pause and reflect on your current situation after reading this chapter. What evidence do you have that you are getting PLC implementation right, and what evidence do you have that you aren't there yet? After reflecting, explore the suggested resources for further study individually or with your teams.

RESOURCES FOR FURTHER STUDY

Step 1: Determine the Essential Learning Target

- Chapter 2 in *Simplifying Common Assessment* (2017) by Kim Bailey and Chris Jakicic (2017)

- Chapter 6 in *Learning by Doing* by Richard DuFour, Rebecca DuFour, Robert Eaker, Thomas W. Many, Mike Mattos, & Anthony Muhammad (2024)

- Chapter 4 in *School Improvement for All* by Sharon V. Kramer and Sarah Schuhl (2017)

Step 2: Set a SMART Goal and Create the Common Formative Assessment

- Pages 121–142 in *Learning by Doing* by Richard DuFour, Rebecca DuFour, Robert Eaker, Thomas W. Many, Mike Mattos, and Anthony Muhammad (2024)

- Pages 19–21 in *School Improvement for All* by Sharon V. Kramer and Sarah Schuhl (2017)

Step 3: Give the Common Formative Assessment

- Chapter 7 in *Learning by Doing* by Richard DuFour, Rebecca DuFour, Robert Eaker, Thomas W. Many, Mike Mattos, & Anthony Muhammad (2024)

- Chapter 5 in *School Improvement for All* by Sharon V. Kramer and Sarah Schuhl (2017)

- Chapter 2 in *Simplifying Common Assessment* by Kim Bailey and Chris Jakicic (2017)

Step 4: Ensure Inter-Rater Reliability

- Page 187 in *Learning by Doing* by Richard DuFour, Rebecca DuFour, Robert Eaker, Thomas W. Many, Mike Mattos, & Anthony Muhammad (2024)

- Pages 37–38 in *Driven by Data 2.0* by Paul Bambrick-Santoyo (2019)

- Chapter 5 in *Simplifying Common Assessment* by Kim Bailey and Chris Jakicic (2017)

Step 5: Share Results

- Pages 178–180 in *Learning by Doing* by Richard DuFour, Rebecca DuFour, Robert Eaker, Thomas W. Many, Mike Mattos, and Anthony Muhammad (2024)

- Page 127 in *Every School, Every Team, Every Classroom* by Robert Eaker and Janel Keating (2012)

- Pages 102–105 in *School Improvement for All* by Sharon V. Kramer and Sarah Schuhl (2017)

Step 6: Develop and Carry Out an Action Plan for Intervention and Extension

- Chapter 8 in *Learning by Doing* by Richard DuFour, Rebecca DuFour, Robert Eaker, Thomas W. Many, Mike Mattos, and Anthony Muhammad (2024)

- Chapter 6 in *Acceleration for All* by Sharon V. Kramer and Sarah Schuhl (2023)

- *Enriching the Learning* by Michael Roberts (2019)

- *When They Already Know It* by Mark Weichel, Blane McCann, and Tami Williams (2018)

Step 7: Capture Team Learning and Make Changes to Instruction

- Page 98 and chapter 4 in *Driven by Data 2.0* by Paul Bambrick-Santoyo (2019)

- Chapter 7 in *Every School, Every Team, Every Classroom* by Robert Eaker and Janel Keating (2012)

4

Providing Time and Support

When a principal asserts that a school is committed to a collaborative culture and helping all students learn but then fails to provide time for teachers to collaborate or for struggling students to receive additional time and support for learning, the claim is recognized as rhetoric rather than reality.

—RICHARD DUFOUR AND MICHAEL FULLAN

Chapter 1 provides the rationale for why schools should function as a PLC, addressing one reason why schools may be unsuccessful in implementing the PLC process. Chapters 2 and 3 explain how teams and singletons prepare and then do the right work in a PLC using the seven-step learning cycle. This chapter addresses the third reason I find educators struggle with PLC implementation—they lack the time and support to work collaboratively and complete the PLC work expected of them. When teachers do not have enough time, or they lack the support they need, they can feel overwhelmed by tasks, including the task of collaboration, which can lead to staff members having a negative outlook concerning the PLC process. Negativity and frustration are normal responses when we feel unable to do what we have been asked to do without the time and support to do it (Muhammad & Hollie, 2012). This negativity is dangerous to school culture.

Time

Teachers need consistent weekly time—approximately one hour per week—to engage in the seven-step learning process well. DuFour and colleagues (2024) state, "Schools and district leaders must provide teachers with time to do the things they are being asked to do" (p. 73). Even if a school gives teachers a half day of collaborative time once per month to do this work, too much time has elapsed between meetings for there to be any continuity or momentum in the seven-step learning cycle. As teams progress in the cycle and become more committed to the process, their need for time each school year will only increase.

In *Learning by Doing*, DuFour and colleagues (2024) provide several strategies for schools to consider as they seek to find time for teachers to collaborate, many of which don't involve any additional staffing, funding, or changes to the master schedule. These suggestions include the following.

- Ensuring common prep time for teachers on the same team within the master schedule
- Adjusting start and end time to schedule team time before or after the school day
- Sharing classes across grade levels to allow each grade level to alternate team time
- Coordinating activities such as watching a movie or meeting with the school resource officer that require supervision rather than a teacher to give teachers time to meet
- Banking instructional time to allow for longer periods of collaboration and converting in-service or faculty meetings to team time

It takes time for teams to work through the seven-step learning cycle. If school administration hasn't worked with the teaching staff to determine what is on a teachers' plates, as described in chapter 2 (page 23), prior to beginning the seven-step learning cycle on campus, leaders should facilitate that activity. If the current number of tasks exceeds the time available, that means there is no time for meaningful collaboration.

Sometimes teachers will say they don't have time, but what they might mean is, *I don't believe this is the best use of my time or I don't think the PLC process is that important.* In these cases, leaders might provide a refresher on the why of PLC (see chapter 1, page 7) to help these educators gain perspective on the importance of meaningful collaboration in a PLC.

Support

While time to do the work is part of the support teams and singletons need to work through the seven-step learning cycle, it is not the only thing they need to do their work well. Educators also need the following support.

- A guiding template for the seven-step learning cycle
- Guiding coalition support
- Celebrations and acknowledgments
- Expected norms and norm checks
- Administrative presence, trustworthiness, and consistency
- Schoolwide foundational pillars
- Monitoring and accountability
- District support
- Balance of task with impact
- Ongoing learning

Each of these supports may represent a departure from the way things have been done previously on campus. If so, it is important for teachers to hear from their administrators that the new emphasis is not a "gotcha," but more of a change in focus. The intent is not to make teachers become defensive or to feel overly surveilled, but for administrators to learn to focus on learning—both student and adult learning. Doing that effectively requires administrators to be tight about certain aspects (such as completion of expected documentation), and loose about other aspects (such as what essential learning targets teams have selected).

TEACHERS TALK

"The templates sharpen our focus to have the right discussions and spend time on things that matter." —Berni D.

"The guidance of the templates helped take our team from unproductive teacher talk to productive conversations that had real impact for students." —Mark S.

"The templates are like the directions for how to play the game." —Abbey S.

A Guiding Template for the Seven-Step Learning Cycle

Teams and singletons should have a simple and easy-to-follow template to guide them, just like training wheels help bike riders get started. Templates "are effective because by simply following the steps, the team stays focused on the right work" (Spiller & Power, 2019, p. 28). Often schools have invested considerable time and effort to ensure collaboration, and leaders need ways to know if that investment is making an impact. In my work with teams, four challenges continue to arise.

1. Teams and singletons lack templates that effectively and simply keep them on track as a PLC.

2. Teachers do not have clear expectations for what they should be producing.

3. Expectations for teams and singletons are not standardized, inhibiting the ability of a school to rapidly share effective processes across the school and provide models that can be replicated.

4. Principals don't know how to monitor the progress and effectiveness of collaborative teams and singletons.

While reflecting on my learning as a principal facing these same challenges, I experienced an "ah-ha" moment when I read these words: the "process of gathering and reviewing team *products* on a regular basis is one of the most effective strategies for monitoring the progress of teams" (DuFour, DuFour, Eaker, & Many, 2010, p. 129, emphasis added).

Products. I recall the word resonating with me, and I began to hunt for examples of them. Richard DuFour and Robert Marzano (2011) wrote the following in *Leaders of Learning*.

When school leaders work with their staffs to create a timeline for anticipated *products*, it helps teams focus on the work to be done. Teams
understand that by a certain date, they are expected to present their list
of essential outcomes, first common assessment, first analysis of student
results from the assessment, and so on. Administrators and teachers alike
must guard against the tendency to view the *products* as a to-do checklist.
The products should serve as primary sources for dialogue among teachers
on the team as well as between the team and the principal. (p. 84, empha-
ses added)

Products were reinforced to me as a key to effective teams; however, I recall being unable
to find streamlined examples of them.

Perhaps you or your teams have great templates or protocols that you use to determine
essential learning targets, set SMART goals, create action plans, and capture the adult learning in the PLC process. If so, those templates can become part of your PLC Dashboard in
place of these templates. If not, the templates that follow might be just what your teams
need to get started—the templates (team and singleton versions) teachers use to guide them
through the seven-step learning cycle in an ongoing, sustainable way. These templates are
tools to keep the cycle on track, especially for teachers with less experience. As Jim Collins
and Morten T. Hansen (2011) point out in *Great by Choice*, "The critical step lay not in finding the perfect program or in waiting for national education reform, but in taking action;
picking a good program; instilling the fanatic disciple to make relentless, iterative progress;
and staying with the program long enough to generate sustained results" (p. 57). The following templates help a team know what to be disciplined about.

Once educators (1) have learned why the school should become a PLC, (2) have the time
to work through the seven-step cycle during the work day for about an hour a week as a team,
and (3) have seen how the four PLC critical questions are answered in the seven–step learning
cycle at the team level, most teams will be ready for the template to help them begin.

The template is not everything a collaborative team should be doing, but like those training wheels on a bike, they help get things going and stay going in the right direction, and
they serve as the primary source of dialogue among the team and between the team and the
school leadership.

Don't make the mistake of thinking that copying a template or a protocol, handing it out
to teams and singletons, and then expecting them to complete the template will ensure the
seven-step learning cycle is being done well. On the contrary, teams will need help. As Spiller
and Power (2019) note, "Simply providing the protocol is a good start, but it is essential that
you work through a protocol with the team initially to explain the purpose and walk them
through the process to ensure effective use" (p. 28).

Having all teams use the same template is important. If teams use different templates, it
is much more difficult for teams new to the process to learn from one another, harder for
the guiding coalition to carry out one of their most important tasks of reviewing and giving
feedback on Essential Learning Target Plans, and more time consuming for administrators

to know how to support struggling teams. A critical concept related to the templates is this: The work is not about filling out templates, but about *facilitating conversations and making decisions as a team or as a singleton that significantly impact students and teachers.*

The Essential Learning Target Plan: Team Template

The purpose of the Essential Learning Target Plan is to capture pertinent information for each essential learning target that will lead to improved student and adult learning. Each team completes one Essential Learning Target Plan for each essential learning target. The template can be printed or kept digitally and is not completed in one collaborative team meeting but gradually over time at three distinct times in the seven-step learning cycle, as detailed in chapter 3 (page 41).

The Essential Learning Target Plan, figure 4.1 (page 84), is intended to effectively guide a team through the seven-step learning cycle by capturing team discussions at the following three times.

1. Prior to teaching the essential learning target

2. After team members have given the common formative assessment to students

3. After team members have implemented interventions and extensions

Several words and phrases are underlined on the template to help educators who are beginning the cycle connect the dots of how the whole template works together. Both this template and the singleton template (figure 4.2, page 85) are available as digital and editable downloads at **www.BrigLeane.com/PLCDashboard**.

The Essential Learning Target Plan: Singleton Template

Singletons utilizing the course-alike on-ramp would use the team template in this chapter, as they would have a common formative assessment with a colleague from a different school. This also applies to singletons who have taken the common content on-ramp, with some caveats as noted in *Singletons in a PLC at Work* (Leane & Yost, 2022; see chapter 5). Singletons who are using the critical friend on-ramp use the template in figure 4.2 (page 85) as the basis for getting feedback from their critical friend.

You will notice that the singleton template is like the team template, as most of the seven-step learning cycle still applies to singletons, with a few noted changes. Once the team or singleton template has been fully filled out and completed, it is not updated again. This document will become a part of the PLC Dashboard (see chapter 5, page 107) as a link and increases in student proficiency are noted on the Team and Singleton tab of the PLC Dashboard as the school year progresses.

Guiding coalitions should find a time where they can share the template with groups of teachers and explain to those teachers how the template is organized into the three parts. In addition, I find it effective to ask teachers to circle two prompts in each of the three parts that they think will help their team. Teachers then share what they have circled with a colleague near them and then share with the group any questions they may have about the template.

Essential Learning Target Plan	**Team:**
Purpose: To Increase Student Learning and Capture Adult Learning	

Information to Agree on Prior to Teaching the Unit		
What is the essential learning target? (Include the standard it comes from.)		
CFA date: [Link to CFA]	What is the success criteria for this assessment? (What score = intervention and what score = extension?)	Date to establish inter-rater reliability:
Date or dates for interventions and extensions in class:		
What is the team SMART Goal? _____% proficient by _____ (end date)		

Action Plan Determined by the Team After the Common Formative Assessment	
Percent proficient after first instruction: _____% proficient	List or a link to students who need more time and support:
What are the intervention plans for students who are not proficient yet?	
What are the extension plans for students who are already proficient?	
What instructional practices got the best results?	

Reflections to Capture After Implementing the Action Plan	
What is the percentage of students currently proficient after the action plan? _____% proficient	After interventions, did the team meet the SMART goal?
What intervention strategies proved to be most effective?	
Document changes to instruction to make in this or future units, common errors, and any other team learning.	
What is the team plan for students who still haven't learned this essential learning target?	

FIGURE 4.1: Essential Learning Target Plan for teams.

Visit **www.BrigLeane.com/PLCDashboard** *to download a free reproducible version of this figure.*

Essential Learning Target Plan for Singletons	Name:
Purpose: To Increase Student Learning and Capture Adult Learning	

Information to Determine Prior to Teaching the Unit	
What is the essential learning target? (Include the standard it comes from.)	

Formative assessment date: [Link to formative assessment]	What is the success criteria for this assessment? (What score = intervention and what score = extension?)

Date or dates for interventions and extensions in class:

What is the SMART Goal?

_____% proficient by _____ (end date)

Action Plan Determined After the Formative Assessment	
Percent proficient after first instruction: _____% proficient	List or a link to students who need more time and support:

What are the intervention plans for students who are not proficient yet?

What are the extension plans for students who are already proficient?

What instructional practices made an impact and got good results?

Reflections to Capture After Implementing the Action Plan	
What is the percentage of students currently proficient after the action plan? _____% proficient	After interventions, did you meet the SMART goal?

What intervention strategies proved to be most effective?

Document changes to instruction to make in this or future units, common errors, and any other learning.

What is the plan for students who still haven't learned this essential learning target?

Who was your collaborative partner, and how did they impact your practice?

FIGURE 4.2: Essential Learning Target Plan for singletons.

*Visit **www.BrigLeane.com/PLCDashboard** to download a free reproducible version of this figure.*

TEACHERS TALK

"Completing this reflection has created in our team a desire to observe one another after comparing results. The strategies we came up with immediately impacted our students." —Abbey S.

"The Essential Learning Target Plan is like a booklet of 'best practices' for our team." —Berni D.

The Three Parts of the Essential Learning Target Plan

In the next section, I will explain each part of the Essential Learning Target Plan and show a sample of that part. Although not perfect, the parts of the Essential Learning Target Plan you will see are a good example to follow, and just like exemplary student work, they help other students know what quality looks like; this Essential Learning Target Plan may help you as well.

Prior to Teaching the Unit

These first two steps of the seven-step learning cycle are captured in the top third of the Essential Learning Target Plan shown in figure 4.3. This template is linked in the PLC Dashboard as part of the expected team products.

Essential Learning Target Plan **Purpose:** To Increase Student Learning and Capture Adult Learning		**Team:**
Information to Agree on Prior to Teaching the Unit		
What is the essential learning target? (Include the standard it comes from.)		
CFA date: [Link to CFA]	What is the success criteria for this assessment? (What score = intervention and what score = extension?)	Date to establish inter-rater reliability:
Date or dates for interventions and extensions in class:		
What is the team SMART Goal? _____% proficient by _____ (end date)		

FIGURE 4.3: Top third of the Essential Learning Target Plan.

The top section of figure 4.3 contains steps 1 and 2 of the seven-step learning cycle and can be completed days, weeks, or even months before a unit begins. Usually, teams complete it a few weeks before a unit begins, and it can be based roughly on dates from district or curriculum pacing guides from the beginning of the school year, if available. Shifts from expected annual pacing guides often happen because of weather-related interruptions, testing taking longer than anticipated, students needing more time on some essential learnings, and many other normal adjustments that teams make. Completing the top part of the Essential Learning Target Plan begins by recording the essential learning target the team is working on. Teams must also create the common formative assessment and provide a link to it so that everyone on the team is clear on the rigor of the common formative assessment from the outset. Teams must then determine the success criteria for the common formative assessment. For instance, a team might say the success criteria for their upcoming common formative assessment is for students to get a 3 out of 4 on a four-point rubric. Students scoring a 1 or 2 would be in the reteaching intervention group, and students scoring a 3 or a 4 would be in the extension group. It also prompts teams to determine dates they plan to do the other steps in the cycle, such as when inter-rater reliability will be established, when the Action Plan (the middle part of the Essential Learning Target Plan) will be determined, and when intervention and extension will take place. Teams also capture the SMART goal. Getting very clear on dates really matters, because as Paul Bambrick-Santoyo (2019) states, "If a plan is made without a specific and well-defined time for action, then it will probably be neglected due to the perpetual competing demand for a teacher's time" (p. 98).

Some teachers fall into the trap of thinking they can wait to decide the intervention date after they grade the assessments. In general, this creates scheduling problems, which makes intervention and extension less likely, and this negatively impacts students. Teachers may not know *who* won't learn the essential learning target after the common formative assessment is given, but they know there will be some, so they should plan for intervention time from the beginning.

Figure 4.4 shows a completed sample of the top third of the Essential Learning Target Plan.

Essential Learning Target Plan		**Team:**
Purpose: To Increase Student Learning and Capture Adult Learning		Grade 7 Math
Information to Agree on Prior to Teaching the Unit		
What is the essential learning target? (Include the standard it comes from.) I can recognize and represent proportional relationships between quantities (7.RP.A.2)		
CFA date: 9/9/25 [Link to CFA]	What is the success criteria for this assessment? (What score = intervention and what score = extension?) 4 or 5 out of 5 correct = extension 3 and below = intervention	Date to establish inter-rater reliability: 9/9/25
Date or dates for interventions and extensions in class: Last twenty minutes of class on 9/15, 9/16, and 9/17		
What is the team SMART Goal? __70__ % proficient by _____9/17/25_____ (end date)		

FIGURE 4.4: Sample top third of an Essential Learning Target Plan.

After Team Members Have Given the CFA to Students

Steps 5 and 6 of the seven-step learning cycle are captured in the middle third of the Essential Learning Target Plan (shown in figure 4.5).

Action Plan Determined by the Team After the Common Formative Assessment	
Percent proficient after first instruction: _____% proficient	List or a link to students who need more time and support:
What are the intervention plans for students who are not proficient yet?	
What are the extension plans for students who are already proficient?	
What instructional practices got the best results?	

FIGURE 4.5: Middle third of the Essential Learning Target Plan.

Teams discuss and complete the middle section of the Essential Learning Target Plan after they have given the common formative assessment, established inter-rater reliability, and teams are ready to share their results. This should take place as soon as possible after giving the common formative assessment—at least within a few days—as teachers need time to grade their assessments and be ready to make an action plan for intervention and extension.

The action plan has five components teams will need to capture.

1. The overall percentage of all students from all teachers on the same team who were proficient after administration of the common formative assessment.

2. A list or link to a spreadsheet showing proficiency skill by skill, student by student. These are the specific results that make up the overall percent proficient.

3. A plan for students who did not yet demonstrate their proficiency on the essential learning target.

4. A plan for students who have already demonstrated their proficiency on the essential learning target and are ready for extension.

5. A determination of which instructional techniques got the best results.

Capturing the instructional practices that got the best results on the common formative assessment is done with the intention of making changes to instruction based on what is working best with similar student groups. For example, a team may focus on what strategies got the best results for their English learners, or what got the best results from students with an IEP. An apples-to-apples comparison prevents team members from saying, "Well, if I had all of the advanced students in my classes, I would have done better, too." Remember that the purpose of comparing results is not to judge one another, but to find out what instructional practices are working so other team members can implement those practices as well. It helps when administrators prompt teachers often to be on the lookout for instructional practices that are getting better results.

In this middle section, teachers record the percentage of students who are proficient on the current essential learning target after initial instruction and before in-class intervention. Teachers should insert a link to a teacher-created spreadsheet to track target by target and student by student who has and who has not yet learned the essential learning target. A digital and editable spreadsheet is downloadable for educators from my website (visit **www.BrigLeane.com/PLCDashboard**).

Acting on these data is the right work of collaborative teams in a PLC; as Sharon Kramer (2015) writes, "Turning data into usable information that can be acted on in a timely manner is what improves schools" (p. 29). Too often, educators overlook this actionable data.

The sample action plan in figure 4.6 shows where on the template teams record their plans for intervention and extension.

Action Plan Determined by the Team After the Common Formative Assessment	
Percent proficient after first instruction: __44__% proficient	List or a link to students who need more time and support: CFA Data by student
What are the intervention plans for students who are not proficient yet? Sept 15–17 • Focused, whole-group instruction for the reteach group—with detailed modeling—using the proportion templates • Guided instruction using gradual release • In small groups, one-on-one instruction for those who need intensive support	
What are the extension plans for students who are already proficient? Choice: Students will have three options—(1) Make a pamphlet for a job that has different price structures (in grade 7 math folder), (2) PowerPoint demo of proportions, or (3) Mr. Christensen's mowing project.	
What instructional practices got the best results? Khan Academy grade 7 proportion video Using daily warm-ups to practice finding unit rate	

FIGURE 4.6: Sample middle part of the Essential Learning Target Plan.

Teams should have already set the date for finalizing the action plan prior to starting the unit. This date, along with several other critical dates pertaining to the seven-step learning cycle, should be pre-planned and put on the Essential Learning Target Plan or added to upcoming team agendas so they are not missed. Teams should document intervention actions as well, such as differentiation within a classroom, trading of students for short-duration intervention at the same time as extension, and perhaps even using some intervention and extension time built into the master schedule that isn't being used for other Tier 2 or Tier 3 interventions.

After Team Members Have Implemented Interventions and Extensions

Teams capture their reflections on the last two steps of the seven-step learning cycle in the bottom third of the Essential Learning Target Plan shown in figure 4.7.

Reflections to Capture After Implementing the Action Plan	
What percentage of students is currently proficient after the action plan? 73% proficient	After interventions, did the team meet the SMART goal? Yes!!—Currently 164 out of 225 students are proficient or above
What intervention strategies proved to be most effective? • Small-group instruction and station activities • Teacher created Quizizz to review skills (in team Unit 3 folder) • Teacher reviewing one on one with paper copy of the test to seek to understand problem • Reviewing previous skills from Eureka grade 6 Module 1 • During remediation, students turning in a product / exit ticket (more structure helped)	
Document changes to instruction to make in this or future units, common errors, and any other team learning. • Students get confused when finding the unit rate from a table and divide x/y instead of y/x. Be explicit, such as, "Do we want to know the miles per gallon with cars or gallons per mile?" Then talk about how the first value goes on top. • When questioning students, use popsicle sticks to randomize who will share their answers to increase engagement. • Students still have trouble reading a graph and finding the unit rate. Use Eureka pages 11–17 for practice. • Students have trouble understanding conceptually what it means to find the unit rate. They need much more practice with this than we thought, even when we thought they knew it. Don't quit early! • Students have trouble relating the unit rate to the context of the problem. When they find the constant, they are not sure what it means. Practice this using text pages 33–34. • Students are unsure how to determine which quantity is the *y* or *x*. Ask district math content specialist for advice. • Develop a third version of the CFA so re-takers don't just memorize answers.	
What is the team plan for students who still haven't learned this essential learning target? On 10/15, 11/11, and 12/4 during the last thirty minutes of class: We will gather students who are still red or yellow on the spreadsheets and remind them that this was an essential target and reteach. We will use peer tutors and give choice to already proficient students like we did before.	

FIGURE 4.7: Sample bottom third of the Essential Learning Target Plan.

In the bottom part of figure 4.7, teams capture the updated percentage of students proficient in the essential learning target after the action plan was carried out. Hopefully, this percentage will be higher than the first time the team gave the common formative assessment. As discussed in step 7 in chapter 3 (page 72), this is where teams and singletons indicate

SMART goal attainment and record effective intervention strategies. Note that strategies recorded here are different than the instructional practices that got the best results during initial instruction.

This section prompts educators to look back at the SMART goal they set to see if they have made it or not. Remember that whether SMART goals are attained or not, the goal is student growth and that the process is getting results on other measures as well.

The next prompt is the ideal place to capture any notes the team does not want to forget the next time they teach the same essential learning target. Notes could include changes that need to be made to the common formative assessment, errors that many students made, timeline adjustments needed next year, or any other team learning.

Finally, the last box asks educators to consider what they intend to do for students who still haven't learned the essential learning target, even after reteaching intervention attempts and reassessment have already been done. This is a window into the need for Tier 2 interventions and a chance to get specific about the plans for those interventions. Remember, teams did not call these "nice to know" targets, but rather essential to know, so regardless of whether the SMART goal has been met or not, students not demonstrating their proficiency on essential learning targets are drowning within reach and need a plan. This is the spot to capture that plan.

The products of the seven-step learning cycle are captured in the Essential Learning Target Plan, which becomes a part of the PLC Dashboard. Figure 4.8 shows a completed Essential Learning Target Plan for a singleton.

Essential Learning Target Plan for Singletons	**Name:** Camilla Clarke
Purpose: To Increase Student Learning and Capture Adult Learning	

Information to Determine Prior to Teaching the Unit	
What is the essential learning target? (Include the standard it comes from.) I can identify the areas of the stage and types of stages. I can justify positions on stage with strong choices with other actors. (CR.2.2 Collaborate: Students will collaborate with a creative team to prepare for a drama / theatre work.)	
Formative assessment date: September 14 [Link to formative assessment]	What is the success criteria for this assessment? (What score = intervention and what score = extension?) At or above 80% = extension; below 80% = intervention
Date or dates for interventions and extensions in class: September 18, 19, and 20	
What is the SMART Goal? __78__ % proficient by __September 30__ (end date)	

Action Plan Determined After the Formative Assessment	
Percent proficient after first instruction: __61__% proficient	List or a link to students who need more time and support: Formative assessment results

FIGURE 4.8: Sample Singleton Essential Learning Target Plan.   continued →

What are the intervention plans for students who are not proficient yet?
On September 18, 19, and 20: Blooket, centers with quiz-quiz-trade activity, extension game with whole class, ships / sailors, racing to corners

What are the extension plans for students who are already proficient?
Choices for September 18, 19, and 20: (1) Create a game for positions on stage to lead a review with, (2) design a set for an arena stage, or (3) make a video with other students explaining stage directions in a creative way.

What instructional practices made an impact and got good results?
Checks for understanding and identifying similarities and differences

Reflections to Capture After Implementing the Action Plan	
What percentage of students is currently proficient after the action plan? __75__% proficient	After interventions, did you meet the SMART goal? No

What intervention strategies proved to be most effective?
Blooket, quiz-quiz-trade, physicalizers

Document changes to instruction to make in this or future units, common errors, and any other learning.
The Areas Game is really good; however, be more specific in the initial play-through to include positions on stage as well, as this will reduce student confusion. Create better parameters for extension activities and more time for quiz-quiz-trade. Seek out other games or activities to review with. Consider guided notes?

What is the plan for students who still haven't learned this essential learning target?
They will get targeted repetitive review in the next unit and learning blocking for the in-class play. Students who are not yet proficient will be pulled aside during the last ten minutes of class on Oct 12 and again on Oct 26 for reteaching and reassessment.

Who was your collaborative partner, and how did they impact your practice?
Angela C. and I share planning periods, so she was my critical friend—we used the critical friend protocol. She spotted several ways I could make the essential learning target clearer to my students and her advice really upped the rigor of my formative assessment.

Guiding Coalition Support

One of the most effective ways the guiding coalition can support teachers in the seven-step learning cycle is by reviewing team and singleton Essential Learning Target Plans and providing feedback, as mentioned in chapter 2 (page 23). While the guiding coalition will not review every Essential Learning Target Plan, it should review two or three exemplary Essential Learning Target Plans at each meeting. When I work with guiding coalitions, I ask the group to pair up and find two "glows" (commendable parts of the Essential Learning Target Plan), and one "grow" (a question the pair has about what is recorded on the Essential Learning Target Plan). I ask a few pairs to share their glows and grows before reviewing another exemplary Essential Learning Target Plan with the same process. As William M. Ferriter, Parry Graham, and Matt Wight (2013) note, "When it comes to developing collaborative products, teachers need support in order to make progress together" (p. 68). One member of the guiding coalition should record aspects of the Essential Learning Target Plans that are done well along with any questions about the Essential Learning Target Plan and communicate back to the team or singleton.

For other Essential Learning Target Plans, pairs of educators on the guiding coalition could be assigned to a specific grade level or subject and be responsible for giving feedback on Essential Learning Target Plans. When a guiding coalition pair finds an exemplary Essential Learning Target Plan, they can share it with administration for the entire guiding coalition to review. Guiding coalition members can also share exemplary Essential Learning Target Plans with their teams to find noteworthy aspects and sections that spark questions. The ensuing discussion among the team allows everyone to see the quality work of other teams and consider how their team could improve. This activity can also take place with the whole staff at staff meetings and should be led by the guiding coalition.

I have observed something almost magical happen when guiding coalitions begin reviewing Essential Learning Target Plans: plans across the campus get much better. I believe this happens for two reasons: (1) teachers learn that someone is looking at their plans, and (2) when teacher leaders examine the exemplary plans of other teams, it helps them understand the expectations and they produce better Essential Learning Target Plans on their own teams.

Teams unable to complete Essential Learning Target Plans are most likely not willing or able to follow the seven-step learning cycle. This is an indication that the team needs some type of support. It could be that an administrator or an instructional coach is needed at meetings, that the team needs more time to work together (additional time during in-services or staff meetings, or through creative ways of finding coverage for their classes for a half or full day), or that the team doesn't yet believe the cycle will be worth their time. In these cases, administration should take lead responsibility to support the team with resources and clarified expectations. Having the input of the guiding coalition as a sounding board to help administrators determine their next steps can be invaluable.

In addition to the Essential Learning Target Plans, the guiding coalition should also review some team common formative assessments and data-tracking spreadsheets to discuss and give feedback either to a specific team or to the school as a whole. Administrators should set up guiding coalition agendas to ensure these tasks are accomplished.

Guiding coalitions that consistently reinforce the importance of the seven-step learning cycle and encourage teachers that they can do the cycle make a significant difference in the overall school success of implementing, leading, and sustaining the PLC process. Likewise, guiding coalition members need to know that the administrators on the guiding coalition are there to support them and that failure is not an option.

Celebrations and Acknowledgments

DuFour and colleagues (2024) affirm the positive impacts that celebrations have on educators. They recommend planning specific celebrations with a clear link to the behaviors leaders are encouraging. Examples of simple celebrations that link clearly to behaviors include the following.

- A principal shows a short, simple, team-created common formative assessment at a staff meeting and then shares how the team is eager to see student results next week. This acknowledges the good work of the team and shows other teachers that common formative assessments don't have to be long and complicated.

- During a faculty in-service day, a guiding coalition member shares a photo of a teacher reteaching a group of students a few days after a common formative assessment for intervention. The faculty members then share with a shoulder partner the ways they intervened for students who are below proficient on a recent common formative assessment.

- An assistant principal shares at a department meeting a screen shot of a team's learning from an Essential Learning Target Plan to demonstrate how important adult learning is to this process. Attendees then share an instructional strategy they now use because of a colleague getting better results on a recent common formative assessment.

- The principal shares a screenshot of a list of student results from a common formative assessment retake that shows many students were initially below proficiency and are now at or above proficiency due to the team's efforts at reteaching.

- When a team completes an Essential Learning Target Plan, the guiding coalition acknowledges them in a small way that raises awareness that they are monitoring and encouraging the work. It doesn't have to be expensive or elaborate; it can be a favorite treat in the teachers' lounge when all teams and singletons have completed at least one Essential Learning Target Plan.

This simple method of finding and celebrating quick wins can make a significant impact on the change process at schools (DuFour et al., 2024; Kramer & Schuhl, 2017). An excellent tool for capturing quick wins is your cell phone. Build the habit of taking pictures of anything related to the seven-step learning cycle as you go about your day. The pictures you take and the stories behind those pictures can significantly impact school culture. When teachers see their work being acknowledged and celebrated, many are inspired. In addition, when teachers see exemplary work from their colleagues, they get a clearer picture of what the work they are also being asked to do looks like, and the samples they see make the work seem more possible.

Some of my colleagues liken our PLC work to the work of an orthodontist. Orthodontists don't look for the perfectly straight tooth and anchor all the other teeth to that tooth. Instead, they use the unaligned teeth to align each other. As teams begin learning the PLC process together by doing it, teachers learn from each other how to do the work through acknowledgment and celebration and grow in their knowledge of how to ensure learning more effectively over time.

Expected Norms and Norm Checks

Many teams are accustomed to identifying norms and understand their importance. DuFour and colleagues (2024) state that *norms* are the "ground rules or habits that govern the group" (p. 80). Norms are the commitments team members make to one another that help them behave in mutually acceptable ways during productive collaboration. I have helped teams create two categories of norms—"norms light" and "norms heavy"—and both are important. *Norms light* help teams clarify the administrative behaviors and attitudes that help the team function best, while *norms heavy* clarify the actions teams must take to increase interdependence in the seven-step learning cycle. A template to help teams create their norms appears in figure 4.9.

To start, teams should reach consensus on a few norms from each of the two categories. For an explanation of the consensus process in a PLC, see "Arrive at Consensus on Consensus" in *Learning by Doing* (DuFour et al., 2024, pp. 36, 40–42). Then, every few

Collaborative Team Norms
Team members:
Date:
Norms light (For example, what commitments will we make for how often we meet, our starting and stopping times, participation, paraphrasing when we want to ensure we understand other perspectives, presuming positive intent, silence is considered disagreement, coming prepared for meetings, looking for ways to celebrate the work, using technology only to support the process, following written agendas, how differing opinions will be handled, and so on):
Norms heavy (For example: How soon before a unit will we create common formative assessments? How soon after formative assessments are given will we grade them? How many formatives will we co-grade to ensure inter-rater reliability? Will we trade papers to grade to remove bias? How long after the assessment will we implement results? How will we document and implement best instructional techniques? For intervention and extension, will we trade students for a day or two for immediate intervention and extension after the CFA?):
When our norms are broken, we will:
We will notify administration when:

FIGURE 4.9: Collaborative team norms template.

*Visit **go.SolutionTree.com/PLCbooks** to download a free reproducible version of this figure.*

months (or more often for struggling teams), teams should conduct a norm check. An ineffective norm check would ask, "How are our team norms going?" Often teachers will say "fine" whether they mean it or not. A more effective norm check happens when team members are asked three questions while the current norms are visible for everyone to see.

1. What is one written norm that is going well?

2. What is one written norm that could be improved?

3. What is one norm our team should add, edit, or eliminate to work through the seven-step learning cycle more effectively?

Facilitators of the norm check can be a team leader, an instructional coach, or an administrator. To facilitate an effective norm check, each teacher should have a sticky note or some way to record their answer to each of the three questions, with the expectation that everyone must write something for each question. Collect the notes between each question and discuss. This support helps teachers acknowledge the good things on the team first, then gives voice to teachers who are frustrated with teammates who are breaking norms but lack the willingness to confront them.

The norm check process creates constructive conflict. Often teams see conflict as a problem to be avoided, but organizational health specialist Patrick Lencioni (2012) reminds us that *constructive conflict* is a healthy attribute of a team. This "benevolent friction" is a sign of team health. The imposters of healthy conflict are artificial harmony on one end of Lencioni's (2012) conflict continuum and mean-spirited personal attacks on the other end. Artificial harmony happens when teachers who disagree in a meeting remain silent, only to share their true thoughts about a team issue behind closed classroom doors or in the parking lot after school. Personal attacks can happen when the conflict embedded within artificial harmony has been left to fester for too long.

The norm check process described here helps teams bring constructive conflict to the surface in a structured way to address issues and avoid personal attacks. When constructive conflict and differing points of view are seen as a sign of health, educators can let down their guard and become even more effective over time.

Figure 4.10 is an example of team norms that have been refined over several years to reflect the exact behaviors team members expect from one another.

Collaborative Team Norms

Grade 7 ELA Team Members: Nancy Noble, Lucretia DeLaTorre, Mona Saad, Venessa Ford, and Josephine Girgis

Date: April 2023

Norms Light:

1. Start Tuesday collaborative time at 9:52 a.m., and end by 10:37 a.m.
2. Be on task, respectful, focused on the idea at hand, and participate in all ways.
3. Paraphrase for understanding and clarification.
4. Be prepared with materials and notes, completing assignments as promised.
5. Differing opinions will be handled by seeking others' thoughts and using majority rules.

Norms Heavy:

1. Create a common formative assessment at least two weeks before giving the test.
2. Common formative assessments must be graded before the next week's data meeting. Stick to the common formative assessment window dates.
3. We will calibrate five assessments (one per teacher) on the document camera before grading to make sure of inter-rater reliability.
4. The day we compare the data, we will complete a best practices plan for intervention and add it to the Grade 7 English Essential Standards document with links where possible.
5. After the common formative assessment, teachers will reteach the concept, while giving students who met and exceeded the standard an alternative assignment, and then provide more targeted intervention strategies for students who are still not proficient.

Source: Hook Junior High School, Victorville, California. Used with permission.
FIGURE 4.10: Example of collaborative team norms.

Administrative Presence, Trustworthiness, and Consistency

When it becomes obvious that a team is not producing the expected products (the Essential Learning Target Plan, common formative assessments, or essential learning target proficiency data), administrative presence is needed at team meetings. Perhaps that team is falling behind because some on the team don't understand the why of the work, some might not know how to do the work, or some might not have the time or support they need to do the work.

For example, if three grade 4 teachers were unable to prepare their Essential Learning Target Plan prior to a unit starting, an administrator would know this by seeing the missing products on the PLC Dashboard, which would prompt the leader to show up at the next team meeting. Based on what they observe during the meeting, the administrator might consider hiring three substitute teachers for a half day to give the team the time they need to do the work that will highly impact the students they serve.

Administrators also give teams and singletons support by asking them questions, which indicate what they and the school value. For instance, when administration sees that a team has a common formative assessment coming up next Thursday, they then check in with the team about how the common formative assessment is going on that Thursday. Principals can ask questions about any aspect of the team's work—via email or in person—sending the message that the work matters. Principals could also periodically ask teams what support they need and then follow up with those requests.

It is important that teachers have trust in their administrators, and that trust takes time to build. This trust is a prerequisite for the accountability measures of the PLC Dashboard. Without it, the presence of an administrator at a collaborative team meeting might feel arbitrary or like micromanagement. Within a trusting atmosphere, the presence of an administrator among a struggling team can be seen as supportive. When administrators are empathetic when challenges arise, they build trust and establish credibility (Muhammad & Cruz, 2019). Leaders build credibility when their actual use of time matches their stated priorities, when they do what they say they are going to do, and when they possess a deep knowledge of how to make the PLC process come alive on campus. This is why it is critical for leaders to learn the seven-step learning cycle and the templates that guide the cycle alongside teachers. Leaders should have empathy for the challenges and struggles teams face. In addition, having a consistent focus and expectations, regardless of who is on what team or what season of the year it is, helps teachers know that administrators value the work they do. This consistency increases trust in the administration and makes teachers more willing to invest time and energy in the process.

In addition to checking in on teams and singletons who are not keeping up with expectations, as evident by the PLC Dashboard, administrators must check in with each team on a routine basis regardless of how well the team is doing. Administrators should meet with each singleton and team frequently to reinforce to teachers that their work around the learning for both students and educators matters, to answer questions, to celebrate accomplishments, and to offer support. At biweekly team meetings, administrators should focus teams on the PLC Dashboard by having it visible and discussing three questions together.

1. How did the next steps your team made from the last check-in go?

2. What do you notice about the current PLC Dashboard for you or your team?

3. What next steps make sense to work on within the next few weeks that, if accomplished, would improve the team's performance as shown on the PLC Dashboard by the next check-in?

Some schools may prefer to keep an ongoing record of administrative check-ins, which would become a record of what each team has accomplished over time. An example of how to keep a record of the answers to the three check-in questions appears in figure 4.11.

Team and Singleton PLC Dashboard Check-In

"Keep it brief and focused on the Dashboard."

Team member names:

Date:

1. How did the next steps your team made from the last check-in go? What are you proud to have accomplished that moved the PLC Dashboard in the right direction?

2. Is the PLC Dashboard up to date for your team? What do you notice about the current PLC Dashboard for you or your team? Are there any successes or challenges in relation to the Dashboard? Also answer, "Are we where we should be?"

Successes:

Challenges:

3. What next steps make sense to work on within the next few weeks that, if accomplished, would improve progress on the PLC Dashboard by the next check-in?

FIGURE 4.11: Team and singleton PLC Dashboard check-in template.

*Visit **go.SolutionTree.com/PLCbooks** to download a free reproducible version of this figure.*

If an administrator (or a delegate, such as an instructional coach) cannot meet with each team once every two weeks for a ten- to fifteen-minute focused discussion based on the three check-in questions, consider setting the goal to meet once every three weeks. That should be possible. If it isn't, school leadership should consider whether all students learning the essential learning targets is really the focus of the school.

Schoolwide Foundational Pillars

Once educators have worked through the seven-step learning cycle several times, the guiding coalition can work with staff to solidify the foundational elements of the PLC school, including developing a shared mission, vision, collective commitments, and goals (DuFour et al., 2024) that support the work.

Mission and Vision

Imagine a school where consensus has been developed over time to establish the agreed-upon mission: To ensure high levels of learning for all students. Staff meetings open with a leader or educator repeating the mission. When schools celebrate staff accomplishments, the celebrations should be within the context of the school's mission. For example, "Because our mission is to ensure high levels of learning for all students, I want to celebrate our grade 10 social studies team who intervened with students within three days of giving their latest common formative assessment." Starting with the agreed-upon mission whenever possible helps everyone keep the main purpose in mind.

A vision is a picture of the future that an organization aspires to become. Imagine a school's vision is that they want to become a model PLC in four years. An alignment question to ask is, "If the proposed vision became a reality, would our mission be more likely to be realized?" In this case, if a school became a model PLC school, it is highly likely that more students would be learning at high levels. An effective vision is something everyone on campus should be able to picture as a reality. Visions typically last for only three to five years, unlike a mission that can be carved in stone. Once a staff has reached consensus on a vision, it should be used in statements, like a mission, to help members of the school know why decisions are being made. For instance, a principal might say, "Because our vision is to become a model PLC, we will be tracking team products on our PLC Dashboard to celebrate accomplishments and determine which teams need more time and support." Or, "Because our vision is to become a model PLC, we will not be able to spend limited staff energy on planning the 5K Fun Run."

At one school where I worked, once teams had worked through the seven-step learning cycle several times and momentum in the process had grown, they were ready to establish their mission and vision. The new mission statement they adopted was: "The mission is to ensure high levels of learning [defined as at grade level or higher] for all students to compete in a global society" (Hot Springs Junior Academy, 2022). Mission statements should be concise and should not change much over time, if at all. Mission statements are the purpose or the reason the school was built. The vision is what a school aspires to become that they are not now. The vision of that school was, "We will become a national model Professional Learning Community school by the end of the 2023 school year." These two foundational pillars set the context for the work to be done, how money and time are allocated, and what is celebrated and confronted. While many school mission and vision statements do little to impact decisions, they can have a profound impact on the culture when properly implemented (Leane, 2018; Covey, 1989).

Collective Commitments

To ensure learning on a campus, educators must be clear on what they are expected to do. As it pertains to the seven-step learning cycle, teacher teams and singletons are responsible for working through the agreed-upon number of Essential Learning Target Plans and following team norms. These types of tasks are called collective commitments; they describe the agreed-upon tasks that educators will do to make the vision become a reality. For instance, a collective commitment could be that each team will work through the seven-step learning cycle a minimum of eight times in the first school year. It could include commitments such as, "We will focus on the seven-step learning cycle during our allotted team time," "Students who are not proficient on common formative assessments will receive support within days," or "Teachers will use the seven-step learning cycle to find ways to make changes to their instruction to get better results for students." Schools do not need many commitments; they should name and commit to those few critical tasks that if not done would jeopardize the vision becoming a reality.

Goals

PLCs must also set goals. These goals should be schoolwide goals, such as achievement results at each grade level on interim and end-of-year assessments. For example, a school might have the goal to improve student achievement in language arts and mathematics by 8 percent at each grade level as measured by the end-of-school-year assessment. Goals can also be around graduation percentages or reducing the failure rate by grade level.

These foundational pillars of the PLC process do not need to be done as the journey is beginning, but they need to be done sometime after teachers have been trained on the seven-step learning cycle and have worked through the cycle several times so that they have enough clarity to know what foundations they are agreeing to support. Like changing the oil in your car, it isn't urgent to set these foundational pillars today or even tomorrow. But if it is ignored over time, the results could be catastrophic. These foundations bring staff together and provide needed alignment so that the school staff share the same overarching fundamental purpose (mission), compelling future (vision), behavioral guidelines (collective commitments), and targets and timelines (goals). *Learning by Doing, Fourth Edition* (DuFour et al., 2024, pp. 45–53) is a comprehensive resource for information about these foundational pillars.

Figure 4.12 provides sample mission, vision, collective commitments, and goals.

Sample Mission, Vision, Collective Commitments, and Goals

Mission: To ensure high levels of learning for all students.

Vision: To become an AllThingsPLC.info nationally recognized Model PLC School by the end of the 2028-29 school year.

Collective Commitments:

1. We will be contributing members of a collaborative team focused on DuFour and colleagues' (2024) four critical questions of learning.

2. We will follow the seven-step learning cycle and document our learning on Essential Learning Target Plans a minimum of eight times this school year.

3. We will establish, follow, and adjust our norms to consistently work more effectively as a team.

4. We will provide immediate, specific, and effective interventions for all students who do not demonstrate their learning on essential learning targets.

5. We will meet at least once per week for at least forty-five minutes and will produce the expected products of the seven-step learning cycle during that time.

6. We will learn and implement many new instructional strategies as a result of our time together.

7. We will keep parents informed of the progress of their children on the essential learning targets.

Goals:

1. Our state assessment data will grow by 6 percent in all tested subject areas each year.

2. We will have a fully functional RTI system in place with clear Tier 1, 2, and 3 structures in place by the 2027–28 school year.

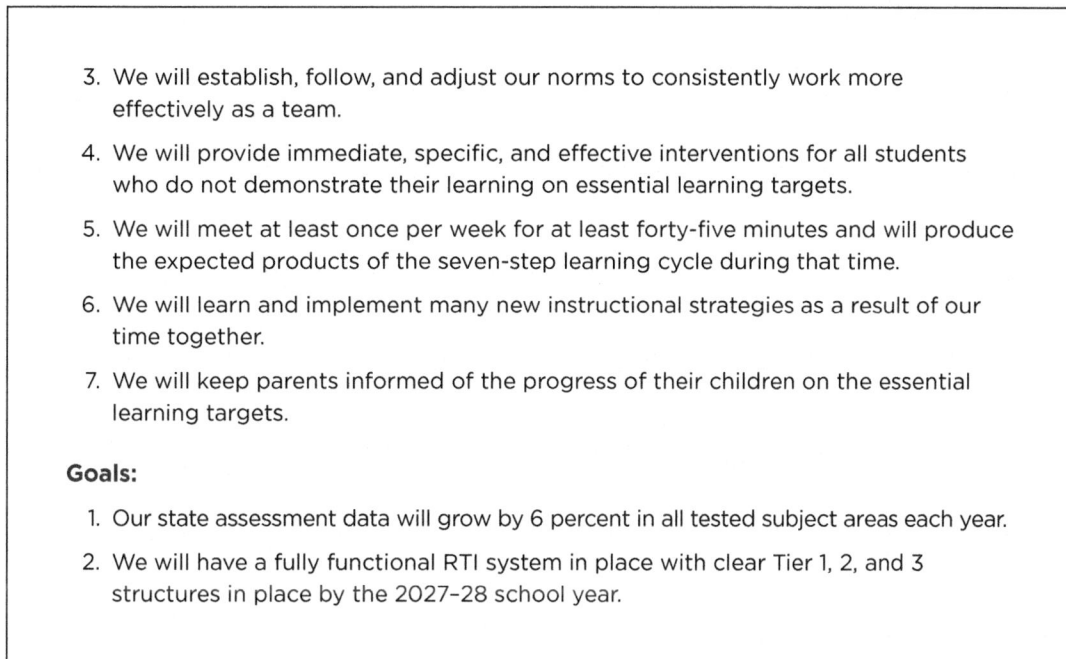

FIGURE 4.12: Sample mission, vision, collective commitments, and goals.

Monitoring and Accountability

How do teachers know what matters to school leaders? They know by what they see leaders doing, saying, spending time and money on, acknowledging and celebrating, questioning, confronting, and, above all, monitoring. To be effective, guiding coalitions and principals must monitor those things related to the mission of learning at the school. The PLC Dashboard (chapter 5, page 107) will give every educator on campus a simple way to monitor team progress. For example, in figure 4.13 an elementary PLC Dashboard indicates the grade 3 team is

struggling to keep up with the expected Essential Learning Target Plan pace. The administration's credibility increases when they address this issue in a respectful way.

How does a busy administrative team give valuable feedback on team products? First, it is critical that the guiding coalition review at least one team product during each meeting as discussed in chapter 2 (page 23) and chapter 4 (page 79). In addition, administrators should consider dividing up the teams and singletons and providing feedback to assigned teams on a consistent basis. Feedback on every Essential Learning Target Plan is not necessary, but no feedback on plans will not

The PLC Dashboard	
Teams and Singletons	**List Essential Learning Target Plans Completed**
Kindergarten	1, 2, 3, 4
Grade 1	1, 2, 3, 4
Grade 2	1, 2, 3, 4, 5
Grade 3	1, 2
Grade 4	1, 2, 4
Grade 5	1, 2, 3, 4, 5

FIGURE 4.13: Sample elementary PLC Dashboard in initiating stage.

move the process forward on campus, either. Feedback could be an emailed question to a team about what essential learning target the team is currently working on, how student proficiency on the target is going, an acknowledgment of progress, or questions about an intervention plan for students. An administrative team could hold a weekly meeting among themselves to share what Essential Learning Target Plan feedback they provided and how to improve consistency of expectations and the quality of feedback.

While some may feel that accountability has a negative connotation, it is worse when it seems that nobody cares. In his book, *Three Signs of a Miserable Job*, Patrick Lencioni (2007) says that irrelevance and immeasurement are two major contributors to dissatisfaction in any job. According to Lencioni (2007), employees need to know that their job matters (relevance) and they must be able to gauge their progress and level of contribution for themselves (measurement). If school or district leaders fail to measure student learning or team progress in the PLC process, it can lead to suffering that could be avoided.

District Support

For a school to become a PLC, strong support to do so from the school district is helpful. This includes superintendents, who clarify the conditions they expect to see in every school within their district. These conditions, adapted from DuFour and colleagues (2016), for districtwide implementation of the PLC process include the following.

- Ensuring every staff member is on a collaborative team or identified as a singleton with a plan for meaningful collaboration
- Ensuring each team and singleton is determining the essential learning targets from each unit of study
- Ensuring each team and singleton have created formative assessments to determine the learning of students on the essential learning targets that have been identified
- Ensuring each team and singleton have used a protocol, such as the Essential Learning Target Plan, to capture planning as it pertains to the four critical questions of a PLC
- Ensuring students who do not learn the essential learning targets are given additional time and support regardless of the teacher to whom they have been assigned
- Ensuring students who have already demonstrated proficiency in essential learning targets are given opportunities to extend their learning
- Ensuring each school is using a method, such as a PLC Dashboard, to track PLC implementation progress
- Sticking with the PLC process as the main district focus for the long term

District administrators should frequently ask themselves and the principals and teachers they support the following questions.

- What are we doing that is helping you ensure every student learns everything your teams and singletons determine to be essential?
- What are we doing that is hampering your efforts to ensure every student learns everything your teams and singletons determine to be essential?
- What changes should we make to ensure every student learns everything teams and singletons on campus determine to be essential?

Soliciting this type of information and acting on it can make a substantial difference, as districts play a pivotal role in the effective implementation of the PLC process on campuses and their support and expectations of the PLC process are vital.

Balance of Task With Impact

While it is critical that teams produce Essential Learning Target Plans, there is a danger if leaders or teams begin to believe that plans are just one more thing to be done. Tying Essential Learning Target Plans to their impact on students, teachers, and the entire school, and connecting Essential Learning Target Plan tasks to the mission or vision of a school impacts the successful implementation of the PLC process on campus (Leane, 2018).

While it is important to frequently acknowledge the products teams and singletons are creating—including Essential Learning Target Plans, common formative assessments, and results spreadsheets, addressing the underlying two purposes (student and adult learning) of PLC work is critical. One way to acknowledge how the work is impacting students is for teachers to name students who didn't initially demonstrate proficiency but did after intervention. This can be done in a team meeting where teachers briefly share students' before and after stories. Hearing about student impact is inspirational.

Additionally, leaders should acknowledge the second purpose, adult learning, often. They can do this in a variety of settings, and it involves asking teachers to share new instructional strategies they now use as a result of the seven-step learning cycle.

The importance of acknowledging the impact the cycle is having on both student and adult learning cannot be overstated and fuels the ongoing work as this invigorates educators.

If the tasks get too much emphasis, they can seem like just another thing to do, and yet if the tasks are neglected, the work of teams can become unfocused and unproductive. Educational leaders should balance the tasks of the team with taking the time to identify the impacts the tasks are having on specific teachers and on specific students.

Ongoing Learning

It is important for educators to consistently be reading and learning as professionals. I have compiled a list of quick reads and key continuums from *Learning by Doing* (DuFour et al., 2024; DuFour et al., 2016) in figure 4.14 (page 104). This list contains page numbers for both the third and fourth edition of this bestseller. These short readings could fit into a staff or department meeting to positively impact school culture while educators learn more about the PLC process together and take away ideas for next steps. Leaders should check in on those next steps to support educator growth and to let them know their personalized next steps matter. This consistency reinforces for teachers that they are making progress in the critical work of shifting from teaching to learning, from isolation to a collaborative culture, and to focus on results (the three big ideas). I recommend some readings to be done once and some annually. Figure 4.14 also includes the main topic the reading addresses and implementation suggestions. These are suggested readings and frequencies; guiding coalitions should make decisions on readings and frequency based on campus needs. Figure 4.14 also lists several key continuums that guiding coalitions should use to rate their PLC periodically, to celebrate progress, and to determine campuswide next steps for improvement.

Reading From Learning by Doing (third or fourth edition)*	Frequency	Main Topic and Implementation Notes
LBD3 pages 9–14 LBD4 pages 13–21	Annually	Three big ideas and purpose: Jigsaw and share out in groups what matters most.
LBD3 pages 20–21 LBD4 pages 27–30	Once	Why ensure learning for all? Share what stood out most in groups.
LBD3 page 78 LBD4 page 87	Once	Why collaborate? Find quotes individually that resonate and share with others.
LBD3 page 127 LBD4 page 163	Once	Clarifying essential learnings: Quick read and discuss with a partner.
LBD3 page 131 LBD4 page 165	Once	Dangerous detours to clarifying essential learnings: Quick read and discuss with a partner.
LBD3 pages 135 (from the top) to 137 (including top paragraph only) LBD4 pages 169–171	Annually	Addresses students with an IEP and the purposes of formative assessment: Read, highlight main takeaways, and share.
LBD3 pages 142–146 LBD4 pages 179–181	Once	Seven reasons for common assessments: Which one stands out to you most? Share with others.
LBD3 pages 150 (part 5)–157 LBD4 pages 190–192	Once	Six tips for common assessment implementation: Which stands out to you the most? Share why with a partner.
LBD3 pages 169–170 LBD4 pages 202–206	Once	Key criteria for targeting interventions: Read and share in small groups what stands out and why.
LBD3 page 173 LBD4 page 210	Once	Why should we intervene when students don't learn? Find quotes that resonate and share with others.
LBD3 pages 178–181 LBD4 pages 215–217	Annually	Nine tips for creating systematic interventions: Which tip stands out to you the most and how will your team implement it?
LBD3 page 185 LBD4 page 220	Annually	Dangerous detours of interventions: What stands out to you the most and why?
LBD3 pages 257–262 (omit 258–260, but this section is good for another activity) LBD4 pages 299–307	Annually	The fierce urgency of doing PLC work now: Find quotes that stand out and share them.
Five Key Continuums LBD3: Pages 16, 80, 128, 151, 176 LBD4: Pages 23, 89, 161, 185, 213	Annually assess	Whole staff or guiding coalition assesses current status. Track growth and develop next steps over time to improve on each key continuum.

LBD4 = *Learning By Doing, Fourth Edition* (DuFour et al., 2024)
LBD3 = *Learning by Doing, Third Edition* (DuFour et al., 2016)

FIGURE 4.14: Quick reads and key continuums from *Learning by Doing.*

NEXT STEPS

Based on what you've learned in this chapter, what two or three next steps will you take to ensure educators have the time and support they need to implement the work they are being asked to do?

Summary

Teachers need time to carry out the seven-step learning cycle and support throughout the process. Without time and support, the process itself is set up to fail at best and could create a toxic school culture at worst. The PLC Dashboard quickly informs leaders which teams and singletons need more time and support and which are progressing as expected so that school leaders can take action.

PAUSE AND REFLECT

Evidence you are getting it right:

- Teams and singletons have about one hour per week for the seven-step learning cycle.

- Many teams and singletons receive specific acknowledgment of their seven-step learning cycle work and how it is connected to the school's mission, vision, collective commitments, and goals.

- Guiding coalition team members review Essential Learning Target Plans and give feedback to teams and singletons regularly.

- Teams update their norms frequently to make them more specific.

- At least one administrator or instructional coach meets with each team and singleton at least every three weeks to discuss successes and challenges.

- Teachers learning and implementing new instructional strategies is seen as a major focus of the seven-step learning cycle.

- Teams get more time and support when they are unable to get the expected team products completed.

- Constructive conflict and differing opinions are evident on teams and seen as a sign of strength.

- All educators on campus are learning and refreshing PLC fundamentals often by reading or visiting other campuses.

Evidence you aren't there yet:

- There isn't time for the seven-step learning cycle.

- Only a few or one team on campus gets recognized for their work.

- Administration does not review Essential Learning Target Plans often.

- Administration hasn't visited with each team and singleton in over a month.

- Teachers cannot think of a new instructional strategy they have implemented.

- Teams and singletons who fall behind are in trouble.

What is a strength from this chapter that may already be going well on campus that could be acknowledged and celebrated?

FOR FURTHER STUDY

- Chapter 2 in *How to Leverage PLCs for School Improvement* by Sharon V. Kramer (2015)

- Chapters 3 and 7 in *Learning by Doing* by Richard DuFour, Rebecca DuFour, Robert Eaker, Thomas W. Many, Mike Mattos, and Anthony Muhammad (2024)

- Chapter 7 in *School Improvement for All* by Sharon V. Kramer and Sarah Schuhl (2017)

5

CHAPTER 5

Implementing the PLC Dashboard

Leaders do more than hope that educators teach the guaranteed and viable curriculum: They establish a process to monitor whether or not students are in fact acquiring the knowledge and skills the curriculum is meant to provide them.

—RICHARD DUFOUR AND MICHAEL FULLAN

Leaders who want to sustain the PLC process over time must consistently focus on ensuring student proficiency of the essential learning targets; we should pay attention to what we care about. But educators are busy and easily distracted by the sheer volume of urgent issues that arise in schools. As the authors of *The 4 Disciplines of Execution* (McChesney, Covey, & Huling, 2012) write, "If important measures are not captured visually, and updated regularly, they will disappear into the distraction of the whirlwind" (p. 75).

By implementing a PLC Dashboard, even an extremely busy administrator can quickly tell how teams and singletons are doing with the PLC process. For example, the administrator looking at the PLC Dashboard page in figure 5.1 (page 108) will see that the grade 8 mathematics team and the music singleton have not completed several Essential Learning Target Plans and seem to be behind the expected pace. Now would be a good time for the administrator to check in with the grade 8 mathematics team and the music teacher during their next team time to see what additional support they may need.

While some schools may be ready to begin a fully functional PLC Dashboard with the team and singleton information tab developed later in this chapter, I recommend administrators initiate the process with more simplicity and build up the process toward sustainability over time. In *Learning by Doing*, DuFour and his coauthors (2024) present continuums that show how the members of a PLC should grow over time—pre-initiating, initiating, implementing, developing, and sustaining. This chapter uses similar stages of development for implementing the PLC Dashboard in a school.

The PLC Dashboard			
A	B	C	D
Teams and Singletons	**List Essential Learning Target Plans Completed**	**List Essential Learning Target Plans At or Above SMART Goal**	**What is your next step based on this PLC Dashboard?**
Grade 7 ELA Team	1, 2, 3, 4, 5	1, 3, 4, 5	Work on Tier 2 interventions for ELTP 2 on Dec 12
Grade 8 ELA Team	1, 2, 3, 4	1, 2, 3, 4	Finish ELTP 5 by next week
Grade 7 Math Team	1, 2, 3, 4, 5, 6	1, 2, 4, 5	Tier 2 interventions for ELTP 3 during WIN time for two weeks
Grade 8 Math Team	1, 2, 3	1, 3	Complete ELTP 4
Grade 7 Social Studies Team	1, 2, 4, 5, 6	1, 2, 4, 5	Complete the reflection on ELTP 3
Grade 8 Social Studies Team	1, 2, 3, 4, 5	2, 3, 5	Tier 2 interventions for ELTP 1
PE	1, 2, 3, 4, 5	1, 4, 5	Get district support for intervention ideas for essential learning target 2
Music	1, 2, 5	5	Complete last section of ELTP 3
STEM	1, 2, 3, 5	1, 2, 3	Plan Tier 2 interventions for ELTP 4

*ELTP = Essential Learning Target Plan

FIGURE 5.1: Sample PLC Dashboard.

Initiating

To introduce your staff to the PLC Dashboard, I recommend beginning with transparency. Consider your reasons for wanting a PLC Dashboard and share those with staff, such as your need for a more streamlined way to know which teams need more support and a way to ensure acknowledgment and celebration of the great work teachers are doing. You might also share that at first in the initiating stage, the guiding coalition—administrators in particular—will be keeping the PLC Dashboard up to date. Initiating the PLC Dashboard sometime after the guiding coalition has worked with the staff on the PLC fundamentals and after the Essential Learning Target Plan has been introduced is preferrable, as communicating all of these at once might be overwhelming for staff.

Constructing the PLC Dashboard

When constructing your PLC Dashboard, begin by listing team names, including singletons, in the first column, column A (figure 5.2). This listing is important so that every teacher is assigned to a team or listed as a singleton, and none are left out. Next, in the second column, column B, record the Essential Learning Target Plans that are complete. All parts of the Essential Learning Target Plan must be finished for teams or singletons to count them as completed. For instance, if a team or singleton adequately fills in all the prompts on the Essential Learning Target Plan except the reflections after the action plan has been carried out, that plan doesn't count as completed. Figure 5.2 shows columns A and B of the PLC Dashboard.

Keep in mind there is flexibility in how column A is set up. Some schools may want to group by grade level, as shown in figure 5.2, or by subject level, as shown in previous chapters of this book.

While most schools I have worked with list the essential learning targets that have been completed (for example, ELT2, ELT3, ELT4, and ELT5), some just keep a count. I prefer listing the targets so that it is obvious which essential learning targets teams have completed and which they have not. A school might also consider labeling each essential learning target with an abbreviated academic content label, such as Fractions 1 or Claims 5. While this may be worthwhile for quick reference for the focus of the essential learning target, the actual description of

The PLC Dashboard	
A	B
Teams and Singletons	**List Essential Learning Target Plans Completed**
Grade 7 English	1, 2
Grade 7 Math	1, 2, 3, 4
Grade 7 Science	1, 3, 4, 5
Grade 7 Social Studies	1, 2, 3, 4, 5
Grade 7 Computers	1, 2
Grade 7 Band	1, 2, 3, 4, 5
Grade 7 Health	1, 2, 4, 5
Grade 8 English	1, 2, 3, 4, 5
Grade 8 Math	1, 3, 4
Grade 8 Science	2, 3, 4, 6

FIGURE 5.2: Initiating PLC Dashboard.

each essential learning target is contained in top part of the Essential Learning Target Plan, so schools should do what works best for them.

After downloading the PLC Dashboard template (available at **www.BrigLeane.com /PLCDashboard**), consider hiding the additional columns until your school is ready for them. When you are initiating the process, the second column will be empty until teams begin to complete and submit Essential Learning Target Plans. Updating the initiating PLC Dashboard could be the responsibility of one person on each team, but the administration has lead responsibility for ensuring it is regularly updated. Within three to four months after beginning, the PLC Dashboard should look like figure 5.2.

You can see in figure 5.2 that many teams are progressing well through the seven-step learning cycle, while some are struggling to keep up. For example, a guiding coalition referencing the PLC Dashboard in figure 5.2 can quickly tell that the grade 7 English team and the grade 7 computers singleton teacher need more support. The grade 8 mathematics team may also need support. It would be wise for a member of the guiding coalition to reach out and see how the seven-step learning cycle is going for that team as well. The grade 8 science team may have also overlooked fully completing Essential Learning Target Plan 1 and may just need a reminder to complete it. There are also many teams and singletons that are keeping up the pace, and those teams should be acknowledged.

When a large California high school with which I was working was starting the PLC Dashboard with their staff, they recorded each team and singleton as they got through each of the three parts of the Essential Learning Target Plan, instead of waiting for the entire plan to be completed before recording it on their dashboard. Breaking the Essential Learning Target Plan into smaller parts helped them identify those who need more support quicker and helped them identify quick wins even faster.

TEACHERS TALK

"The PLC Dashboard is like a shortcut menu, with access to everything we need. The investment is worth the return!" —Jesus P.

"The PLC Dashboard brings our team to the same focus. It has brought my team together." —Nancy N.

"All of the info is in one place! I can now know what my students will need to be ready for next year, too!"—Mona S.

"The PLC Dashboard takes the guesswork out of what our team is supposed to do. It keeps everyone accountable and lets us know what's next." —Erica M.

Leading Indicators and Lagging Indicators

The initiating PLC Dashboard captures leading indicators that teams have a great deal of control over. Leading indicators are different from lagging indicators, which become known much later. Lagging indicators are the measurements of results you are trying to achieve in the long term (McChesney, Covey, & Huling, 2012) and are typically captured in schoolwide goals, one of the foundational PLC pillars (DuFour et al., 2024). Lagging indicators, such as mid-year Northwest Evaluation Association (NWEA) measures of academic progress (MAP) testing results or end-of-year state testing results, are the measures that the leading indicators are intended to impact. In other words, if teams and singletons work diligently through the Essential Learning Target Plans and get increasingly more students to proficiency on those essential learning targets, middle and end-of-year testing results should be increasing as well. Lagging indicators are not always as responsive to the immediate work of the team, yet they give educators feedback on how well the leading indicators are at getting the desired results.

This initiating PLC Dashboard will help get the process going, get some quick wins, and likely not overwhelm the administration as the process is getting started on campus. Ideally, the initiating phase should last approximately three to four months and should be updated frequently before adding additional steps.

In addition to the digital PLC Dashboard, I recommend a large visual as well, such as a magnetic whiteboard in the staff meeting room or other prominent place where teachers will see it. When a team completes an Essential Learning Target Plan, they might put a school emblem, such as a mascot sticker or a graduation cap with the essential learning target number, on the whiteboard during a staff meeting to celebrate plan completion and quickly identify missing plans.

Understanding Perspectives

Figure 5.3 provides a discussion framework for learning the perspectives of educators throughout the school. The information administrators and the guiding coalition gain from the answers to the questions can help them determine if the school is ready for the next stage.

Questions to Guide the Work of PLC Dashboard Implementation: Initiating Stage

To assess the progress at this stage, ask educators the following questions.

1. How do we know how well teams and singletons are getting through the seven-step learning cycle?

2. In what ways is the work of teams and singletons celebrated as it pertains to completion of Essential Learning Target Plans?

3. What feedback are teams and singletons receiving after submitting Essential Learning Target Plans?

4. In what ways is team progress working through the seven-step learning cycle being monitored on a frequent basis?

5. In what ways are assessment results being used to improve instructional strategies?

6. How do we know what time and support teachers need to be successful at the seven-step learning cycle?

7. In what ways are other initiatives being limited so that teachers have enough time and energy to devote to the seven-step learning cycle?

FIGURE 5.3: Questions to guide the work of the PLC Dashboard initiating stage.

*Visit **go.SolutionTree.com/PLCbooks** to download a free reproducible version of this figure.*

Implementing

Once schools have gotten their two-column initiating PLC Dashboard up and running and are able to keep up with giving teams and singletons feedback on their Essential Learning Target Plans, they should be ready to unhide the third column to begin to measure if teams are getting results in student achievement. Administrators should discuss the update with staff to share details of the new column. Assure teachers that SMART goal attainment is not necessarily the goal; rather, the goal is the academic growth of students and teacher learning, which may or may not mean attaining a SMART goal. Encourage teachers that you would rather have a team set a high SMART goal and have a rigorous common formative assessment or formative assessment, and not meet that SMART goal, than have a team set an easy-to-attain SMART goal, or a nonrigorous common formative assessment or formative assessment, and have no growth results on lagging indicators take place. The goal of the new column is for everyone on campus to begin considering intervention needs and to celebrate teachers when they meet challenging SMART goals that they set.

Figure 5.4 shows the third column, column C, which identifies the Essential Learning Target Plans that are at or above the team-determined

The PLC Dashboard		
A	B	C
Teams and Singletons	**List Essential Learning Target Plans Completed**	**List Essential Learning Target Plans At or Above SMART Goal**
U.S. History	1, 2, 3, 4	2, 3, 4
World History	2, 3, 4	2, 3, 4
Biology	1, 2, 3, 4	1
Chemistry	1, 2, 3, 4	1, 2, 3

FIGURE 5.4: Implementing PLC Dashboard.

SMART goal for each essential learning target. When you begin this stage and reveal this column, each team should update it with their most recent results.

This new column indicates if students are learning what they were expected to learn, as determined by the teacher teams and singletons. Often when teams are starting the seven-step learning cycle on campus, SMART goal attainment reflected in this column can feel like a guessing game, since many teams aren't sure how high to set their SMART goals. For this reason, some guiding coalitions will defer monitoring this column until teams have had some practice implementing SMART goals. Like the Essential Learning Target Plan completion column, listing the essential learning targets that are at or above the team SMART goal is helpful so that only those essential learning targets that are below the SMART goal need to be checked in the future as interventions get more and more students to proficiency.

Let's analyze the example in figure 5.4. Many teams are completing Essential Learning Target Plans, but biology is struggling to get the students to the team-determined SMART goal on Essential Learning Target Plan 2, 3, and 4. This team may need more support in how to effectively intervene for students on prior essential learning targets that they have already taught and assessed this school year. Or perhaps the biology team is feeling the pressure to get through the curriculum and doesn't believe they have time to pause to ensure learning on the essential learning targets. This is a departure from the first big idea of a PLC, a focus on learning, where teams focus not just on teaching the curriculum, but also on students learning what is taught. The PLC Dashboard highlights the issue with biology; after the guiding coalition notes the issue, they should seek to understand why the team needs support. The data in columns B and C are leading indicators over which teachers have a great deal of control. If they attend to these columns, the result should be higher levels of learning for students on the lagging indicators.

The implementing PLC Dashboard should be visual beyond the spreadsheet as well. For example, one secondary school with a mission of ensuring "Graduation for All" made a bulletin board with a listing of each team and singleton on campus. The administration put a cutout of a graduation cap for each Essential Learning Target Plan a team completed and each SMART goal they attained, as shown in figure 5.5.

Source: Cabot Freshman Academy, Arkansas. Used with permission.
FIGURE 5.5: Sample bulletin board PLC Dashboard.

Balancing Rigor and Meeting SMART Goals

School leaders should remember that there must be a balance between the need for high rigor on formative assessments and the desire to meet SMART goals. It would be wise for leaders to celebrate a team that sets a challenging SMART goal with a rigorous formative assessment, even if the students don't meet the SMART goal after multiple interventions. If such acknowledgment does not routinely occur, some teachers might "game" the process and simply lower all SMART goals or lower the rigor of formative assessments.

The following are some scenarios to illustrate how an administrator, instructional coach, or a guiding coalition could respond after reviewing the information in the implementing PLC Dashboard stage. These assume that the seven-step learning cycle began at the beginning of the school year.

- **Scenario 1:** It is October, and a high school computer apps team has three Essential Learning Target Plans completed, with three that have met the SMART goal.

- **Response 1:** This team may be doing great, or maybe their essential learning targets or common formative assessments are not very rigorous. It would be appropriate to celebrate the successes of this team and to ask questions about the rigor or the success criteria of the common formative assessments.

- **Scenario 2:** It is February, and a grade 3 team has six Essential Learning Target Plans completed and one where the percent currently proficient meets or exceeds the team's SMART goal.

- **Response 2:** The grade 3 teachers need to focus on interventions for students who have not yet shown proficiency on previous essential learning targets. Tier 2 intervention needs to take place. This could involve meeting with this team and helping them schedule an upcoming date and time for students who are not yet proficient on a previous essential learning target to receive targeted additional time and support—and then be reassessed on another version of the common formative assessment.

- **Scenario 3:** It is March, and a grade 8 U.S. history team has two Essential Learning Target Plans completed and two where the percent currently proficient exceeds the team's SMART goal.

- **Response 3:** These teachers need to get through more essential learning targets. Administrators should consider joining this team at their next meeting and working with them to get the top portion of the Essential Learning Target Plan completed for an upcoming essential learning target. Administration should have known this team was behind and reacted well before March, a benefit of the visibility of team progress on the PLC Dashboard; however, it is the interpretation of the PLC Dashboard this example demonstrates.

The implementing stage should result in more wins to acknowledge and celebrate, and should last another three to four months, with frequent updates to the Dashboard before revealing additional columns.

Understanding Perspectives

Figure 5.6 (page 114) provides a discussion framework for learning the perspectives of educators throughout the school. The information administrators, instructional coaches, and the guiding coalition gain from the answers to the questions can help them determine if the school is ready for the next stage.

**Questions to Guide the Work of PLC Dashboard
Implementation: Implementing Stage**

To assess the progress at this stage, ask educators the following questions.

1. How do we know which teams and singletons need more support in getting through the seven-step learning cycle?

2. In what ways is the work of teams and singletons celebrated as it pertains to meeting the SMART goals as set out in the Essential Learning Target Plans?

3. What feedback are teams and singletons receiving after submitting Essential Learning Target Plans?

4. In what ways is student learning being monitored on a frequent basis?

5. How do we know that proficiency on an Essential Learning Target Plan in one teacher's class would be the same in another teacher's class?

6. How do we know that assessment results are being used to improve instructional strategies?

7. In what ways are students who are struggling getting additional time and support to learn the team- or singleton-determined essential learning targets?

8. In what ways is our school celebrating students who didn't at first demonstrate proficiency, but did after action plans made the difference?

FIGURE 5.6: Questions to guide the work of the PLC Dashboard: Implementing stage.

*Visit **go.SolutionTree.com/PLCbooks** to download a free reproducible version of this figure.*

Developing

Once the school has been working with the implementing PLC Dashboard for long enough to feel that it is manageable, schools are ready to add an extra step that further focuses educators on the PLC Dashboard in the developing stage (see figure 5.7, page 115).

Keeping Track of Next Steps

Columns D and E represent one method of keeping track of team and singleton next steps to improve the PLC Dashboard. Column D is the place to record the date of the biweekly check-in to set the next steps listed in column E. The purpose of column E is to record a next step or two that will improve either column B (Essential Learning Target Plans completed) or column C (Essential Learning Target Plans that are at or above the team- or singleton-determined SMART goal). This is accomplished by administration facilitating a meeting with each team and singleton through the biweekly check-in (discussed in chapter 4, page 79).

In the developing PLC Dashboard stage, administrators should communicate to staff the changes to the Dashboard and why the two new columns are important. Gradual release of responsibility of the PLC Dashboard from administration to teams is an important step for teams to take ownership of pacing of essential learning targets and balancing the pace with student needs to be proficient in essential learning targets sooner rather than later.

The PLC Dashboard				
A	B	C	D	E
Teams and Singletons	List Essential Learning Target Plans Completed	List Essential Learning Target Plans At or Above SMART Goal	Date of Current Next Step	What is your next step to improve column B or C?
Kindergarten	1, 2, 3, 4, 5, 6	1, 2, 5	Feb 4	Tier 2 interventions for ELTP 3 on Feb 27 in class
Grade 1	2, 3, 4	2, 3, 4	Feb 3	Complete ELTP 1 by Feb 21
Grade 2	1, 2, 3, 4	1	Jan 14	Tier 2 interventions for ELTP 2 on Feb 20
Grade 3	1, 2, 3, 4	1, 2, 3	Jan 21	Finish the team reflection on ELTP 5
Music	1, 2, 3, 5	1, 2, 3	Feb 2	Complete the missing sections of ELTP 4
PE	3, 4, 5, 6	1, 2, 3, 4, 5	Feb 5	Reflect on and document ELTP 1 and 2

*ELTP = Essential Learning Target Plan

FIGURE 5.7: Developing PLC Dashboard.

Understanding Perspectives

Figure 5.8 provides a discussion framework for learning the perspectives of educators throughout the school. The information administrators and the guiding coalition gain from the answers to the questions can help them determine if the school is ready for the next stage.

Questions to Guide the Work of PLC Dashboard Implementation—Developing Stage

To assess the progress at this stage, ask educators the following questions.

1. How do we know that teams and singletons are focused on improving the PLC Dashboard to subsequently improve both student and adult learning?

2. In what ways are school leaders interacting with teams and singletons?

3. What feedback are teams and singletons receiving after submitting Essential Learning Target Plans?

4. In what ways are students who did not yet demonstrate proficiency on essential learning targets from this school year still getting additional assistance to become proficient on those skills?

5. In what ways are records being kept of team and singleton next steps in improving the PLC Dashboard?

6. In what ways are new instructional strategies teachers are implementing being recognized by school leaders?

FIGURE 5.8: Questions to guide the work of the PLC Dashboard: Developing stage.

*Visit **go.SolutionTree.com/PLCbooks** to download a free reproducible version of this figure.*

Sustaining

The PLC Dashboard has one final component that provides a way to efficiently monitor the PLC process and sustain it over time. This component is found in the Team and Singleton Information tab.

Creating and Using the Team and Singleton Information Tab

While the PLC Dashboard lets everyone know how teams are doing, it doesn't represent all the information that effective leaders should collect and monitor. The Team and Singleton Information Tab keeps track of additional aspects of an effective PLC, just like a basketball coach needs more information than is shown on the scoreboard (the PLC Dashboard) to optimize the team. This expanded record of the teams serves three purposes.

1. It provides common storage of team products.
2. If staff members leave or files are misplaced, the record of team learning and planning for the next school year is not lost.
3. The information from the Team and Singleton Information tab is used to update the PLC Dashboard.

Figure 5.9 is a sample Team and Singleton Information Tab. Column A is a list of teams and singletons, just like the PLC Dashboard. Columns B, C, and D list the names of the teachers who are members of each team, when teams meet, and have links to team norms. Completed entries let leaders know what to celebrate and blank entries indicate which teams and singletons need more time and support.

Column E stores an annual list of essential learning targets, usually as a hyperlink to a document such as the one shown in figure 5.10 (page 118) from a grade 7 English team. When just starting the PLC process on campus, teams and singletons may be unable to produce an annual list like the one shown in figure 5.10, which is why all columns of this tab are not typically developed until the sustaining stage. Even a partial list is beneficial for teams in the beginning. However, once the PLC process is more familiar and staff have been doing the work longer, an annual list should be available at the start of the school year so that teachers get closer and closer to a guaranteed and viable curriculum—Marzano's (2019) number one factor for student achievement. To reinforce this critical element, leaders could acknowledge those who do know their annual essential learning targets and share samples such as the one in figure 5.10 to help other teams understand the expected product.

In figure 5.9, column F, the final year-long column, holds a link to a team calendar that shows where each of the essential learning targets fits into the school year for each team. Figure 5.11 (page 118) is an example of a high school mathematics team with eight essential learning targets for the year; the team will go through the seven-step learning cycle for each essential learning target. The team has planned dates for each essential learning target, increasing the likelihood that these essential skills are guaranteed for every student regardless of the teacher assigned and viable because they fit into the calendar.

	A	B	C	D	E	F	G	H	I	J
		Year Long					Essential Learning Target 1		Essential Learning Target 2	
	Team and Singletons	Members	Team Meeting Times	Norms (link)	Yearly List of Essential Learning Targets (link)	Calendar (Year at a Glance; link)	Essential Learning Target Plan (link)	Percent Currently proficient (total of all classes)	Essential Learning Target Plan (link)	Percent Currently proficient
	Kindergarten	Brown, Ackerman, Jones, Bowen	8:50 Tues	Norms	K ELTs	K Calendar	K ELT1	44%	K ELT2	78%
	Grade 1	Mills, Maeker, Cuddemi, Twadell, Spiller	9:30 Mon	Norms	Grade 1 ELTs	Grade 1 ELT Calendar	1 ELT1	74%	1 ELT2	81%
	Grade 2	Ahner, Owens, Kanold, Yost	10:10 Tues	Norms	Grade 2 ELTs	Grade 2 ELT Calendar	2 ELT1	93%	2 ELT2	89%
	Grade 3	Marrillia, Roberts, Keating, Friziellie	10:50 Wed	Norms	Grade 3 ELTs	Grade 3 ELT Calendar	3 ELT1	77%	3 ELT2	61%
	Grade 4	Hall, Andrews, Sonju, Gobble, Schuhl	11:40 Thur	Norms	Grade 4 ELTs	Grade 4 Calendar	4 ELT1	83%	4 ELT2	93%
	Grade 5	Wheatley, Bailey, Nielsen, Hansen, Schmidt	1:50 Thur	Norms	Grade 5 ELTs	Grade 5 ELT Calendar	5 ELT1	71%	5 ELT2	80%
	PE	Hassan	12:15 Mon	Norms	PE K-5 ELTs	PE Calendar	PE ELT1	87%	PE ELT2	28%
	Music	Kuller, Vander Els	2:40 Mon	Norms	Music ELTs	Music Calendar	M ELT1	93%	M ELT2	85%
	STEM	Ritz, Cruz	1:30 Tues	Norms	STEM ELTs	STEM Calendar	S ELT1	89%	S ELT2	78%

*ELT = Essential learning target.

FIGURE 5.9: The Team and Singleton Information Tab.

Annual essential learning targets: Grade 7 English

1. Analyze the development of a theme over the course of a text. RL.7.2

2. Understand and identify the components of a compound-complex sentence. L.7.1B

3. Determine the explicit meaning of a text. RL.7.1

4. Draw inferences from a text. RL.7.1

5. Cite several pieces of evidence to support explicit and inferred meaning. RL.7.1

6. Develop the topic with relevant facts, definitions, concrete details, quotations, and/or other information and examples. W.7.2.B

7. Distinguish between relevant and irrelevant evidence. RI.7.8

8. Introduce claim(s), acknowledge alternate or opposing claims, and organize the reasons and evidence logically. W.7.1.A

9. Determine an author's perspective in a text. RI.7.6

10. Determine an author's purpose in a text RI.7.6

11. Paraphrase information from sources. W.7.7

Source: Hot Springs Junior Academy, Arkansas (2022). Used with permission.

FIGURE 5.10: Sample annual essential learning target list.

Grade 9 Mathematics Team Calendar 2025–2026 School Year							
Essential Learning Target	Unit Begins	CFA	Inter-Rater Reliability	Action Plan Meeting	Reteach Window	Retake CFA	Finalize Tier 1 Data and Reflection
1 Polynomial Expressions	Aug 15	Sep 13	Sep 13	Sep 16	Sep 19–22	Sep 22	Sep 26
2 Solving Equations	Sep 26	Oct 11	Oct 11	Oct 18	Oct 20–25	Oct 25	Oct 28
3 Function Notation	Oct 31	Nov 9	Nov 9	Nov 15	Nov 16-Nov 30	Nov 30	Dec 6
4 Linear Functions	Nov 30	Dec 14	Dec 14	Dec 16	Dec 16-Jan 10	Jan 10	Jan 13
5 Graphing Systems	Jan 17	Jan 31	Jan 31	Feb 3	Feb 6–8	Feb 8	Feb 10
6 Exponential Functions	Feb 21	Mar 3	Mar 3	Mar 8	Mar 9–15	Mar 15	Mar 27
7 Radicals	Mar 27	Apr 6	Apr 6	Apr 11	Apr 12–18	Apr 18	Apr 24
8 Quadratic Functions	Apr 19	May 10	May 10	May 14	May 15–21	May 21	May 28
Math Results Tracking Link							

FIGURE 5.11: Sample team calendar of the year.

Administration sets up the Team and Singleton Information Tab, including inserting links to the Essential Learning Target Plan blank template, and then shares the links across campus. As teams and singletons send year-long team product links to administration, they insert those links into the spreadsheet, with administration taking lead responsibility for ensuring this is completed. In some schools, teams and singletons may have more access and higher expectations for inserting links, but the key is that administration must ensure it is happening. When first starting out, some teams may not have their yearly list of essential learning targets and are simply deciding them as they go. Leaving this cell blank indicates teams and singletons have yet to complete this work. However, all teams should have norms, as well as some calendar dates for when the learning cycle steps are taking place, and those should be linked.

Next to the year-long columns in figure 5.9 (page 117) are the essential learning target columns. Each essential learning target column has two subcolumns. The first of the two columns is to hold a hyperlink to the Essential Learning Target Plan for each essential learning target. The second column for each essential learning target is a place for teams and singletons to update the percent currently proficient for each essential learning target. The team or singleton updates this column each time an additional intervention takes place that increases the percent proficient, even months after the initial teaching of that essential learning target have passed. It is important to note that while teams do not update Essential Learning Target Plans once they have been completed, they do update the percent currently proficient column as more Tier 2 student interventions occur and more students become proficient. This part of the PLC Dashboard indicates where student needs are the greatest—which essential learning target has the most students who need Tier 2 support. Figure 5.9 shows that the kindergarten team and the PE singleton should be giving more Tier 2 support on the essential learning targets that are currently low. The spreadsheet template repeats these two columns for each essential learning target up to sixteen essentials skills. If additional columns are needed, they can be easily copied and pasted.

When administrators meet with teams and singletons, they will most likely use both the PLC Dashboard as well as the Team and Singleton Information tab to display more detailed information on the team. Communicating the intent of this step will be important to teachers and could include such rationale as the need to capture team and singleton products and the legacy they have built so they are not lost when teachers leave or forgotten over the summer.

While schools should adjust any of the tabs to better suit individual school needs, it is important that the guiding coalition get to see how teams are progressing frequently. This positive accountability helps everyone know what is monitored, celebrated, and addressed.

The intent of the PLC Dashboard is to illuminate progress or lack thereof. When leaders make a habit of reviewing the Dashboard and taking action on what it reveals, they are able to discover issues and address them before too much time has passed. For example, imagine a dashboard that shows essential learning target 1 to be at 23 percent proficiency, but the team is currently working on essential learning target 4. This is an indication to the principal to address the low proficiency percentage by asking, "I see the low proficiency on essential learning target 1. Your assessment must have good grade-level rigor. How can I support you in scheduling a Tier 2 intervention on that essential learning target?"

Understanding Perspectives

Figure 5.12 provides a discussion framework for learning the perspectives of educators throughout the school in the sustaining stage.

Questions to Guide the Work of PLC Dashboard Implementation—Sustaining Stage

To assess the progress at this stage, ask educators the following questions.

1. How do we know that every teacher on campus is accounted for on our Team and Singleton Information Tab on our PLC Dashboard?

2. How do we know that the current status of student proficiency for each essential learning target has been updated?

3. In what ways are team norms routinely checked to see if they are effective?

4. In what ways is the school addressing the problem of not all students being proficient on every team or singleton determined essential learning target?

5. How is the PLC Dashboard impacting student achievement at our school?

6. In what ways are our PLC records kept over time so that team and singleton learning is not lost?

7. How can you tell which teams need more time and support by looking at the PLC Dashboard?

FIGURE 5.12: Questions to guide the work of the PLC Dashboard: Sustaining stage.

*Visit **go.SolutionTree.com/PLCbooks** to download a free reproducible version of this figure.*

Celebrating the Wins

One of the principles of effective change is to celebrate wins early and often. When the guiding coalition has determined team configurations in the first column, they should acknowledge that win with the whole campus. When teams are beginning to identify their annual list of prioritized essential learning targets, that win should be acknowledged as well. Let's say all grade-level teams on an elementary campus have completed their team norms except one grade level. If the administration or the guiding coalition celebrates that the majority of teams have submitted their team norms by showing a screenshot of the team names and norms column, in my experience, the team with the missing norms will quickly submit theirs.

A word of caution: The PLC Dashboard gives administrators significant information about teams that could be used to punish those teams or singletons who are falling behind. The intent of the PLC Dashboard should not be connected to rewards or punishment. Author Daniel Pink (2009) encourages leaders who work with knowledge workers, such as teachers, to avoid systems that become "carrots and sticks" but instead to offer educators a sense of their progress in worthy endeavors, like having more students learn more of their team-determined essential learning targets through this process. The PLC Dashboard is about shifting our focus from teaching to learning and believing that teachers are capable and ready to make that shift.

For example, if the PLC Dashboard indicates one team is significantly behind other teams in the number of Essential Learning Target Plans completed, administration will know this and can provide more time and support, perhaps by finding additional time for the team to meet. When other teams see teams and singletons who are behind being treated positively and supported, it will help improve trust.

A school might even consider having a quick celebration like donuts in the staff lounge or a dress-down day in the beginning stages for milestones that are met, such as when each team has fully completed one Essential Learning Target Plan. Keep the acknowledgments fun and focused on celebrating the progress, instead of using the PLC Dashboard to punish.

In addition, celebrate schoolwide progress. To determine where the school is from pre-initiating to sustaining, guiding coalitions can use The PLC Dashboard Continuum (figure 5.13, page 122) to mark progress and determine next steps. Leaders can use this tool to gather information from teams or from the school as a whole. For example, ask teachers to highlight or check phrases that are true, and then use the unhighlighted phrases in the same column or any of the columns to the right as potential next steps for team and schoolwide improvement planning. The guiding coalition might consider getting teacher ratings of where they see the school overall on the continuum and then comparing the teacher ratings to the guiding coalition's or administrators' perspectives.

Ongoing Action Items

There are several ongoing critical actions for teams and singletons, administrators and coaches, and for guiding coalitions. These actions appear in figure 5.14 (page 123).

NEXT STEPS

Based on this chapter, list two to three next steps you will put into action to improve your PLC Dashboard so that more students and educators are learning more.

Summary

Starting the PLC Dashboard with a simplified version allows educators to learn and grow in the PLC process without being overwhelmed at the beginning. It helps teams and singletons rise to a higher standard that they are capable of attaining. The PLC Dashboard isn't about rewards and punishment but about sharpening the focus and allowing everyone to see the progress a school is making in the very worthwhile pursuit of increased student and teacher learning. When educators know why they are doing this work, how their work is measured on the PLC Dashboard, and that they have the time and support to accomplish their work, change will happen.

The PLC Dashboard Continuum

Purpose: To measure the current conditions of starting and sustaining the PLC Dashboard on campus and to develop next steps

Process: Highlight or check phrases that are true. Find an unhighlighted phrase in the same or next column to the right to do next.

Pre-Initiating	Initiating	Implementing	Developing	Sustaining
☐ Educators know the four critical questions of learning and the three big ideas of a PLC.	☐ Teachers know what team they are on for collaboration.	☐ Teams and singletons are getting feedback on their ELTPs by members of the guiding coalition.	☐ Teams and singletons document and take steps to improve the PLC Dashboard.	☐ The school archives team and singleton work on the Team and Singleton Information Tab, including team norms, yearly list of ELTs, and a calendar of where they fit into the school year.
☐ Educators can explain many reasons why the school is working to become a PLC.	☐ Singletons know which on-ramp they will use for collaboration.	☐ The staff see the PLC Dashboard as a source of celebration and an indication of teams who need and receive more support.	☐ Administration facilitates meetings with teams and singletons at least every three weeks.	
☐ Educators have clarity about the two purposes of a PLC: (1) Students mastering essential learning and (2) Teachers learning new instructional strategies.	☐ Teachers know how to use the template to record their progress through the seven-step learning cycle.	☐ Teachers regularly maintain the rigor of the standards in their formative assessments, even if teams and singletons are not meeting SMART goals.	☐ Teachers throughout the school can (1) name several instructional strategies they now use as a result of the seven-step learning cycle, and (2) name multiple students who have benefitted by receiving additional time and support on ELTs.	☐ The proficiency of each essential learning target for each team and singleton is monitored and up to date.
☐ Teachers know the seven-step learning cycle.	☐ The guiding coalition has set up an initiating PLC Dashboard.	☐ Tier 2 intervention is seen as needed because teams throughout the campus have lists of students who need additional time and support on the ELTs.		☐ ELTPs are linked and can be accessed.
☐ A guiding coalition of administrators and teacher leaders has been established.	☐ The guiding coalition is beginning to learn together about the mission, vision, collective commitments, and goals that support the PLC process.		☐ Schoolwide consensus has been achieved on the mission, vision, collective commitments, and goals.	☐ The Team and Singleton Information Tab is frequently used to determine Tier 2 needs.
☐ Educators throughout the building know the purpose of the PLC Dashboard.				☐ Acknowledgments and celebrations pertaining to the PLC Dashboard are frequent on campus.

*ELTP = Essential Learning Target Plan

FIGURE 5.13: The PLC Dashboard continuum.

Visit go.SolutionTree.com/PLCbooks to download a free reproducible version of this figure.

Ongoing Actions for Teams and Singletons

- Make the current essential learning target progress visible in every classroom.
- Do monthly norm checks.
- Work through the Essential Learning Target Plan approximately one time per month.

Ongoing Actions for Administrators and Coaches

- Update the PLC Dashboard.
- Join teams at least every three weeks as they do the work, more often for struggling teams.
- Maintain an attitude of support, not compliance: "We are in this and learning this together."
- Acknowledge the great work of teams and singletons as it relates to any of the seven steps.
- Celebrate instructional strategies that teachers are learning.
- Celebrate specific student success stories that are a result of the seven-step learning cycle.
- Monitor Essential Learning Target Plan completion using the PLC Dashboard and be present with teams and singletons who are unable to complete expected Essential Learning Target Plans.

Ongoing Actions for the Guiding Coalition

- Meet at least every two weeks, for at least forty-five minutes per meeting.
- Review the PLC Dashboard at each meeting.
- Discuss what is working and what isn't pertaining to the seven-step learning cycle.
- Give feedback to teams and singletons on their Essential Learning Target Plans and find exemplary parts to share at staff meetings or in other schoolwide communications.
- Learn together and deliver professional development to the rest of the staff.

FIGURE 5.14: Ongoing action items.

PAUSE AND REFLECT

Evidence you are getting it right:

- Teachers know why the school is using the PLC Dashboard, and it is seen as an aid to accomplishing the mission of the school.
- Educators update the PLC Dashboard frequently.
- Within seconds of viewing the PLC Dashboard, it is obvious which teams and singletons need more support.
- Students who do well on common formative assessments are likely to do well on interim and end-of-year assessments as well.

- Teachers are hungry for information on how well students are doing on essential learning targets.
- Teams and singletons are celebrated and acknowledged often based on completion of tasks from the PLC Dashboard.
- SMART goals help bring together general education, special education, and support teachers, such as English language development teachers.
- Teams and singletons who are falling behind on the dashboard are viewed as being under-supported.
- Teams and singletons are getting closer to sticking with their annual calendar and list of essential learning targets with each passing school year.

Evidence you aren't there yet:

- The PLC Dashboard has not been updated in weeks or longer.
- The guiding coalition is neither looking at nor discussing the current PLC Dashboard at each meeting.
- Educators are told to fill out a template but are unclear on why it matters—they just know that it will be tracked.
- The PLC Dashboard looks great, but students are not growing on lagging measures, such as NWEA Map, STAR, or other interim assessments or end-of-year summative assessments.
- Teams and singletons who are falling behind due to circumstances outside of their control feel like they are in trouble.

What is a strength from this chapter that may already be going well on campus that could be acknowledged and celebrated?

RESOURCES FOR FURTHER STUDY

- Chapter 1 in *The 4 Disciplines of Execution* by Chris McChesney, Sean Covey, and Jim Huling (2012)
- Chapter 4 in *Cultures Built to Last* by Richard DuFour and Michael Fullan (2013)
- Chapter 4 in *Leaders of Learning* by Richard DuFour and Robert Marzano (2011)

E

Putting It All Together

*One of the most damaging myths about school leadership is that the
change process, if managed well, will proceed smoothly.*

—RICHARD DUFOUR, REBECCA DUFOUR, AND ROBERT EAKER

Richard DuFour doesn't sugar coat the difficulties of implementing the PLC process when
he points out the damaging myth that a well-managed change process will proceed smoothly.
Instead, he clearly states that the change process is stormy and full of unexpected challenges,
but, despite this, it is exciting, it is the right work, and it impacts educators and students in a
profound way. Throughout this book, I have made a case for why becoming a PLC matters,
how a seven-step learning cycle and template help guide teams and singletons, and how to
use the PLC Dashboard to determine educator progress. The PLC Dashboard is deceptively
simple and yet is the main tool for helping educators see which teams and singletons are
making progress, which are achieving their SMART goals, and which need more time and
support. While these tools are helpful at focusing educators on the PLC process, no worthwhile change process will proceed smoothly, and it will take consistent, focused time. Like a
fitness routine, diet, or financial goal, the success of this process will be determined by your
commitment level, the positive focus it receives, and perseverance.

My hope is that you now have enough information to get the PLC process started and
to sustain it over time; however, this does not mean that doing only the steps listed in this
book implies completion of the ongoing PLC process. In addition to the resources listed
throughout this book, you will most likely need to delve much deeper into other PLC topics
to sharpen processes and grow students and educators even more, reinforcing the "ongoing"
part of the definition of a PLC. In addition, teachers will occasionally struggle and need to
be reminded of why they are focusing on learning instead of just teaching, and why they are
being asked to do this work collaboratively. Teams will struggle from time to time, and when
new teachers join teams, team dynamics will change. Teams will need assistance with how to
grow even further in the process, and they will need more time to do this work at a higher

level with each passing school year. And while the mission of the school should remain the same, the vision of what the school should become will need to be adjusted periodically as school visions become school realities.

While in the U.S. Coast Guard, one of my jobs was to navigate our ship to our intended destination with the collaboration of the navigation team. If our ship stayed on the same heading and didn't make small course corrections along the way, we could end up miles away from where we were trying to go. It reminds me of how small course changes can have a profound impact over time in schools. I am not asking principals and teacher leaders to change who they are and how they like to operate most of the time. What I do suggest are small changes in what principals and teacher leaders do with the percentage of time they can give to this work around organizing the school to (1) ensure students learn the essential learning targets and (2) ensure adults, the teachers, are learning as a result of this process as well.

Perhaps you have implemented the steps in this book and end-of-year assessments reveal that student achievement has not improved. That will happen from time to time, and while the templates in this book are helpful, until teachers actually make instructional changes, there is little chance for different results. Effective leaders should often ask teachers, "What instructional changes have you made as a result of the seven-step learning cycle?" There should be multiple instructional changes that teachers can list. In addition, when assessment results are not as desired, allow that disappointing feedback to provide pressure for teams to make necessary changes on the essential learning targets they have chosen, the rigor level of their common formative assessments, and the success criteria the team has set. These are ways to stay on the PLC course and make necessary course corrections.

In addition, remember that not every positive result is quantitative. Answering the following questions can be helpful and can serve as a source of encouragement when achievement data takes a dip.

- Are teachers becoming better educators with each passing year because of the PLC process?
- In what ways are new teachers being supported and less likely to give up because of their team?
- In what ways is equity growing on campus because students are learning the same essential learning targets regardless of the teacher they have been assigned to?
- In what ways is hope growing in teachers because undersupported students are becoming more successful?
- Are more students learning more of the team- and singleton-determined essential learning targets than ever before?

There are many ways to measure results, and while student scores are often the most evident, they are not the only way to mark progress. When educators fully submit to the process, results will follow, though not necessarily every year nor always immediately. Like Jim Collins' (2001) Stockdale Paradox in *Good to Great*, when you are doing the right work, the results will come eventually. Finally, knowing why you are doing the work can help you weather the inevitable storms of our profession.

The processes outlined in this book are intended to guide teams in the right work. They are not something else to do; they are the right things for educators to be doing. I encourage you to trust the process, because if you get it right, so many other elements will fall into place. New teachers will feel valued. Meaningful collaboration will increase. Experienced teachers will be able to pass on their legacy. Academic achievement will be realized. Hope in and for your students will grow.

And whether you do this process at a high level or not, you are an educator and will be working hard regardless. As Robert Eaker and Janel Keating (2012) remind us:

> Let's face it, the vast majority of faculty and staff work very hard, and they get tired. Working hard and being tired is simply part of an educator's life. The key to effective leadership is to make sure faculty and staff are working hard and getting tired by doing the right things! This is the difference between working hard and being frustrated, or working hard and feeling fulfilled due to the fact that more kids are learning more. (p. 40)

You are already working hard, so get organized to ensure every student learns everything your teams and singletons say is essential; it makes our great work more fulfilling.

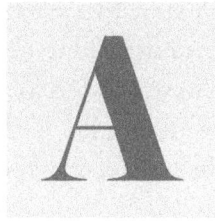

A

Frequently Asked Questions

What if the collaborative team chooses essential learning targets poorly?

This happens. When teams start out, they might choose essential learning targets that are too easy, too hard, or simply the wrong skill, but with reflection and guidance, they will get better. The key is that they get to choose. They will need that ownership to be committed to the professional growth adjustments they will make, and to have the tenacity to stick with the student intervention process. The same applies to singletons.

Does every unit of study have to have an essential learning target?

Not necessarily. There may be units that teachers are simply going to "teach, test, and hope for the best." The important thing is that teacher teams don't get so many essential learning targets going that they can't properly intervene to ensure the learning. Not everything taught is essential, so some concepts just need to be introduced. It is better to start small and do the process right than to have too many essentials to track and intervene and not do any of them well.

This could also happen with a small but required unit, or when a team is just beginning the seven-step learning cycle and doesn't yet have the time or skills needed to keep up with the collaborative team process. However, if a team cannot determine an essential learning target with any unit of study, they must ask themselves why they are teaching that unit at all.

How do you determine the appropriate level of rigor?

This is best started by unpacking the standards as a collaborative team to determine rigor. Additionally, a sound question to ask one another on the team is, "Would proficiency on this essential learning target be a good indicator of proficiency in this subject or standard?"

When do teams determine the essential learning target in a unit?

Before a unit begins. Collaborative teams need to be clear on the essential learning target, have developed a SMART goal, and have created a common formative assessment prior to a unit to ensure the team members are headed in the same direction so students have a guaranteed curriculum regardless of the teacher to whom they are assigned.

What if a team or singleton determines more essentials in a school year in a class than can fit into the seven-step learning cycle with the time available?

This often happens, especially when schools are beginning the PLC journey and they aren't as adept at working through the seven-step learning cycle. For instance, let's say a team has identified eighteen essential learning targets in a year for a grade 8 social studies curriculum, but with only forty-five minutes per week to meet, they believe they can only get through ten essential learning targets. In this instance, I recommend the team select the ten that are spaced out enough with their timing to allow the team to work through the seven-step learning cycle when these ten are taught. It would be ideal for all essentials to make it through the seven-step learning cycle, but it is better to do the process well and get more student and adult learning than to have too many essential learning targets and do none of them well.

The key is to find the sweet spot where there aren't so many essential learning targets that the team gets frustrated or so few essential learning targets that precious collaboration time is underutilized.

Shouldn't SMART goals always be met 100 percent of the time since we are talking about *essential* learning targets?

No. While one of the three big ideas of the PLC process is learning for all, we know that despite our best efforts at great in-class instruction and systematic intervention, there will be some students who do not learn what the team decided was essential. You will check your SMART goal set by the team at the bottom of the Essential Learning Target Plan to see if the goal was met. You will most likely be reaching higher and higher levels each year as your team members learn from one another.

Should all SMART goals end at the end of the school year?

No. Just as it is important to have annual goals, like overall student growth on end-of-year assessments, it is also important to have short-term goals along the way to focus teams, build interdependence, and have accomplishments that can be celebrated.

Should teams set their SMART goals low at first?

No. The seven-step learning cycle is intended to eliminate ineffective teaching practices. If the goals are set too low, then almost any teaching practice might work, but that is not what is best for students. Goals should be stretch goals, and even if they are not reached, they should push collaborative teams and singletons to improve over time. This might happen in a school where fear of not meeting a SMART goal exists. This is a cultural problem that must be addressed where it exists.

Can there be different versions of the common formative assessment?

Yes. For instance, in mathematics, some common formative assessments are very short. Teams would want several versions to reduce cheating or simply memorizing answers. In ELA, teachers can use short stories or excerpts that differ. The key is that the level of rigor the team has determined stays the same with each version of the assessment.

Should the common formative assessments be long?

Since the evidence that feedback matters to student achievement is clear (Hattie, 2009), the longer the common formative assessment, the longer it takes to get the feedback to students. The closer educators can give feedback at the time of the assessment, the more impact they have on student learning. Some highly effective common assessments are short assessments that teachers give to students as an exit ticket. When possible, try to avoid formal assessments that can produce anxiety, require lots of in-class time for students to do them, and take longer to grade and return to students.

What if a teacher is absent the day a common formative assessment is scheduled to be given?

It depends on who the substitute is and how well they can ensure the common formative assessments are administered in alignment with team expectations. If the conditions can be met, the sub should give the common formative assessment. If not, it might be best to postpone until the regular classroom teacher returns. This is a situation where teams need strong communication and must have grace with one another while still sticking to the planned dates to the best of their ability.

How do you ensure inter-rater reliability if the assessment is multiple choice?

The short answer is that you don't, because in those types of assessments, the answers are either right or wrong. However, teams should ensure they have balanced assessments, where some items can be multiple choice, but some should also be constructed response or performance assessments, such as an essay or a project.

Do other experts agree with the number of essential learning targets teams should eventually have?

Mike Mattos and his coauthors (2016) and Kramer and Schuhl (2017) recommend teacher teams select between sixteen to twenty-four essential standards (which often have several learning targets per standard) per school year, recognizing that identifying fewer standards is more effective than having too many. While I believe this is a good goal to build up to over time, the total number chosen will depend on the time available to collaborate, the experience of the team at working through the cycle, the number of essential learning targets per standard, and the team's or singleton's ability to keep up with the seven-step learning cycle documentation. The key is for teachers to keep the work doable with the time and energy available.

Are there other terms that mean the same thing as inter-rater reliability?

Other similar terms that some might use include *calibrating grading* or *co-grading*. The important point is that teachers on the same team must see proficiency and nonproficiency the same way, otherwise when they come together to share results with the intent of finding out which instructional practices are working the best, the results will not provide the information the team is seeking.

How do primary grade teachers establish inter-rater reliability for students who take assessments that must be orally completed by a teacher?

In situations like this, teachers could have several students video recorded while the assessment is being administered, prior to the date planned for the majority of the students to be assessed. The video would then be shown to the teacher team to determine whether the student is proficient. Inter-rater reliability would need to be established prior to any of the teachers assessing their own students. One teacher might say the student is not proficient because the student didn't get the answer right at first, but then self-corrected. Another teacher may believe that self-correction counts. Which teacher is right? This is a decision the team will have to reach.

When the administration collects student common formative assessment results, don't teachers worry that the varying results will be used against them?

Leaders must let teachers know that results of common formative assessments in this process will not be used in teacher evaluations. If low trust exists between teachers and the administration, administrators might require that all student and teacher names be removed but still expect the percentage results for the teachers on the team. Teachers on the team would know who got the best results, but the administration would not. Fear simply must not be part of the process.

What do you consider to be some of the keys to starting this process?

When starting, keep the process doable and share quick wins. If teachers have multiple subjects to prepare for, like many elementary teachers, or multiple preps, like many secondary singletons, have those teachers find an essential learning target from the curriculum in just one class in the next month. When leaders find an educator who has selected their first essential learning target, acknowledge it to the whole staff as another example of the great things going on. Find a team that sets a rigorous SMART goal and share it out as a celebration.

Does selecting essential learning targets mean teachers don't have to teach the rest of the standards?

No. Teachers still teach the standards, give quizzes and tests, and grade student work, but only essential learning targets go through the seven-step learning cycle. Teams agree to work hard to ensure the learning of the essential learning targets, intervene on those several times at Tier 1 and 2, and use the results of the formative assessments as the basis of adult learning.

Should teachers put formative assessment results in the gradebook?

The purpose of grading is to communicate, not to punish or to reward. Whether teachers enter formative assessment results into the gradebook or not is a decision for them to make. However, remember the purpose of communicating. Regardless of the decision, it would also be appropriate to over-write low student grades with higher grades after students have been retaught and their proficiency goes up on the essential learning targets.

What do you do if one teacher has hundreds of students and another teacher only has one class?

Teachers should compare the percentage of students who are proficient, regardless of the number of students they have. This allows the team to determine which instructional techniques are getting the best results, regardless of the number of students a teacher has been assigned.

Are results shared outside of the team?

In general, I recommend giving access to the skill-by-skill and student-by-student results on the common formative assessments among the team and to administration. Access to that data usually does not need to be shared beyond those two groups.

What if one teacher has most of the honors students and another teacher has more struggling learners?

While it is certainly helpful for teachers to be assigned similar heterogenous groups of students, as it pertains to the number of students who are high, medium, and low performing, to then be able to compare results, often that is not feasible due to scheduling constraints. In these situations, teachers should compare students who share similar demographics, such as English learners, or students with an IEP, or non-honors students not on an IEP. Any of these similar group results could be useful for finding out which instructional practices seem to be working best for these and other student groups.

Additionally, when it seems that the sharing of proficiency results will not be producing changes to the way teachers are teaching, perhaps due to the significant difference in the abilities of the students assigned to a particular teacher's class, a critical purpose of the process is lost. To ensure educators are learning from each other, a team may switch to having some sort of preassessment and then compare which teacher grew students the most from the preassessment. While there is some debate about preassessments possibly producing feelings of failure in students who haven't been taught the material, teachers who set the context and reduce the fear factor for students can most likely make preassessment work just fine. The key is that the process is producing adult learning.

What if the school does not have a common intervention time?

I recommend working to change that; however, there are some other ways that students who did not learn what was essential can get assistance. Consider working with a small group of students who did not pass the common formative assessment during regular class time while the rest of the students do some extension work. Another option is to pair up students who passed the common formative assessment with students who did not for a practice session. This helps struggling learners get feedback quicker from a classmate, as student-to-mentor ratios are 1:1. In addition, teachers can sometimes trade students among other teachers who teach at the same time for short durations, where one teacher extends the learning for those who passed while the other teacher conducts an intervention. Remember that there must be intervention and reteaching at Tier 1, which should be taking place in class before the end of the unit. This is different from Tier 2 intervention, where months may have passed and yet some students still haven't demonstrated their proficiency. Some call this Tier 2 time WIN time—What I Need time—indicating that extension and intervention are taking place based on student proficiency.

What if a teacher on the collaborative team is trying something completely new, like a student-centered learning environment, and their results aren't as good as their colleagues?

Often, teachers want to try new teaching techniques—and that is a good thing! When this happens, there often is an implementation dip where results will drop as the teaching technique has not been perfected. One tip is to only select teaching techniques that are research based to begin with. In addition, sometimes the means to an end can become more important than the end itself. This is a risk. For instance, let's say a teacher has heard only a few details about the power of a more student-centered learning environment and decides without much professional development to instantly put the students more in charge of their learning. If the results on the common formative assessment show that this teacher did worse than the other teachers who are using a more traditional approach, it could be due to the implementation dip. If, however, after several attempts, the results continue to be worse, at some point the evidence clearly shows that the teacher should utilize an approach that is getting better results or get more training on instructional strategies.

What if the teacher who got the best results doesn't really know what instructional strategy yielded those results?

Teachers who get the best results should at a minimum be given the opportunity to share what they think worked best. If that teacher isn't sure what made the difference, they should be asked about other things they routinely do that impact student learning, including the relationships they build with students or important communication with parents. Teams might also consider that members could observe the teacher to see if they can identify the strategies responsible for the results.

What if none of the teachers on the team got the best results, but everyone's results were pretty close?

When there isn't much of a difference between results, teams should still record any team learning to include what changes they should make in the next unit or when the same unit is taught the next school year. They should also record any other notes the team wants to remember, including changes they should make to the common formative assessment. This might also be a time to determine if the rigor of the assessment matched the rigor of the standard.

What if everyone on the team got extremely low results?

This is an ideal situation for the team to seek outside assistance. That assistance could come from campus administration, any instructional coaches on campus, or district subject matter specialists who can help the team get better results. The team might also consider studying the matter themselves by reading a book about the practice they are trying to improve or seeking online resources that are effective.

What if someone with access unintentionally messes up the PLC Dashboard?

Google Sheets has a version history—the icon on the webpage looks like a clock—and it allows a campus to go back to a time when the PLC Dashboard was correct.

Do all teams have to use the same Essential Learning Target Plan template?

The short answer is yes, because if every teacher is using the same template, any teacher on campus can see how other teachers are attempting to do the same thing, even if they are in a different subject. Some schools may choose to edit the Essential Learning Target Plan to better fit their own needs, which schools should do.

Do the templates change after the first year?

Yes, but they stay very similar with a few minor changes. In the Essential Learning Target Plan for years two and beyond, there should be a reflection regarding the previous year's Essential Learning Target Plan. Also included is a prompt to look back at the final percent proficient so the new SMART goals stretch the team. In addition, it prompts teams to examine the effective instructional strategies the team documented and discuss implementation of those strategies. An editable version is available for download at **www.BrigLeane.com/PLCDashboard**.

Our school already has a template we are using and like. Do all teams and singletons have to use the guiding templates from this book?

No. If you are already using another template, such as Janel Keating's TACA template, Mike Mattos' Essential Standards Chart, or any similar template that guides educators through the PLC process at the team level, substitute your already-successful template for my Essential Learning Target Plan in this book, and track team and singleton progress with your template through your PLC Dashboard. Just make sure all educators are using the same or similar templates.

What if teams can't get along?

All teams will struggle at times, but some teams seem to struggle more than others. If teams are getting the expected work done, it is probably alright to leave the problems alone; however, if the problems of the team are preventing the team from doing the work expected of them collaboratively, they will need the support of increased administrative presence to assist them, seek to understand the problems, and help determine solutions.

How long does it take to sustain the PLC process on campus?

This obviously depends on the culture of the school and the level of support that educators receive. However, it is reasonable that a school could get to a sustainable stage in the PLC process in three to four years, as long as the process has been consistently encouraged, funded, coached, celebrated, and evaluated.

Should a district have a PLC Dashboard?

The short answer is "it depends." If a district has a dashboard, it can feel to schools that they are serving the district, when it should be districts supporting schools. If the dashboard is only at the school level, then when district administrators look at the school's dashboard, it should help them ask questions of the school or the team with a supporting mindset. The dashboard is intended for leaders at any level in the school or district to know which teams and singletons need more time and support and to take action on that information.

References and Resources

Aldeman, C. (2022). Why are fewer people becoming teachers? [Blog post]. *Education Next.* Accessed at www
.educationnext.org/why-are-fewer-people-becoming-teachers on March 5, 2024.

Ainsworth, L. (2013). *Priority standards: The power of focus.* Accessed at www.larryainsworth.com/blog
/priority-standards-the-power-of-focus on March 19, 2024.

Bailey, K., & Jakicic, C. (2017). *Simplifying common assessment: A guide for professional learning communities
at work.* Bloomington, IN: Solution Tree Press.

Bambrick-Santoyo, P. (2019). *Driven by data 2.0: A practical guide to improve instruction* (2nd ed.). San
Francisco: Jossey-Bass.

Chenoweth, K. (2017). *Schools that succeed: How educators marshal the power of systems for improvement.*
Cambridge, MA: Harvard Education Press.

Clear, J. (2018). *Atomic habits: Tiny changes, remarkable results: An easy and proven way to build good habits
and break bad ones.* New York: Avery.

Collins, J. (2001). *Good to great: Why some companies make the leap…and others don't.* New York: HarperCollins.

Collins, J., & Hansen, M. T. (2011). *Great by choice: Uncertainty, chaos, and luck: Why some thrive despite them
all.* New York: HarperCollins.

Conzemius, A., & O'Neill, J. (2013). *The handbook for SMART school teams: Revitalizing best practices for
collaboration (2nd ed.).* Bloomington, IN: Solution Tree Press.

Cottingham, B. W., Hough, H. J., & Myung, J. (2023). *What does it take to accelerate the learning of every
child? Early insights from a CCEE school-improvement pilot.* Stanford, CA: Policy Analysis for California
Education. Accessed at https://edpolicyinca.org/sites/default/files/2023-12/r_cottingham-dec2023.pdf
on April 1, 2024.

Covey, S. R. (1989). *The seven habits of highly effective people: Powerful lessons in personal change.* New York:
Fireside.

Croft, A., Coggshall, J. G., Dolan, M., Powers, E., & Killion, J. (2010). *Job-embedded professional development:
What it is, who is responsible, and how to get it done well.* Accessed at https://learningforward.org
/wp-content/uploads/2017/08/job-embedded-professional-development.pdf on March 5, 2024.

DuFour, R. (2015). *In praise of American educators: And how they can become even better.* Bloomington, IN:
Solution Tree Press.

DuFour, R., DuFour, R., Eaker, R., Mattos, M., & Muhammad, A. (2021). *Revisiting Professional Learning Communities at Work: Proven insights for sustained, substansive school improvement*. Bloomington, IN: Solution Tree Press.

DuFour, R., DuFour R., Eaker, R., & Karhanek, G. (2010). *Raising the bar and closing the gap: Whatever it takes*. Bloomington, IN: Solution Tree Press.

DuFour, R., DuFour R., Eaker, R., & Many, T. (2010). *Learning by doing: A handbook for Professional Learning Communities at Work* (2nd ed.). Bloomington, IN: Solution Tree Press.

DuFour, R., DuFour R., Eaker, R., Many, T., & Mattos, M. (2016). *Learning by doing: A handbook for Professional Learning Communities at Work* (3rd ed.). Bloomington, IN: Solution Tree Press.

DuFour, R., DuFour R., Eaker, R., Many, T., Mattos, M., & Muhammad, A. (2024). *Learning by doing* (4th ed.). Bloomington, IN: Solution Tree Press.

DuFour, R., & Eaker, R. (1998). *Professional Learning Communities at Work: Best practices for enhancing student achievement*. Bloomington, IN: National Educational Service.

DuFour, R., & Fullan, M. (2013). *Cultures built to last: Systemic PLCs at Work*. Bloomington, IN: Solution Tree Press.

DuFour, R., & Marzano, R. J. (2011). *Leaders of learning: How district, school, and classroom leaders improve student achievement*. Bloomington, IN: Solution Tree Press.

Eaker, R. (2020). *A summing up. Teaching and learning in effective schools and PLCs at work*. Bloomington, IN: Solution Tree Press.

Eaker, R., & Keating, J. (2012). *Every school, every team, every classroom: District leadership for growing Professional Learning Communities at Work*. Bloomington, IN: Solution Tree Press.

Eaker, R., Keating, J., Hagadone, M., & Rhoades, M. (2021). *Leading PLCs at work districtwide: From Boardroom to Classroom*. Bloomington, IN: Solution Tree Press.

Eaker, R., & Marzano, R. (2020). *Professional Learning Communities at Work and high reliability schools: Cultures of continuous learning*. Bloomington, IN: Solution Tree Press.

Eaker, R. (2020). *A summing up. Teaching and learning in effective schools and PLCs at work*. Bloomington, IN: Solution Tree Press.

Ferriter, W. M., Graham, P., & Wight, M. (2013). *Making teamwork meaningful: Leading progress-driven collaboration in a PLC at Work*. Bloomington, IN: Solution Tree Press.

Fullan, M. (1993). *Change forces: Probing the depths of educational reform*. London: Falmer Press.

Hanson, H., Torres, K., Yoon, S. Y., Merrill, R., Fantz, T., & Velie, Z. (2021). *Growing together: Professional Learning Communities at Work generates achievement gains in Arkansas*. Portland, OR: Education Northwest. Accessed at https://educationnorthwest.org/sites/ default/files/plc-at-work-impact-evaluation.pdf on April 1, 2024.

Harvard Business Review. (2023). *HBR guide to executing your strategy*. Boston: Harvard Business Review Press.

Hattie, J. (2009). *Visible learning: A synthesis of over 800 meta-analyses relating to achievement*. New York: Routledge.

Hattie, J. (2015). *What works best in education: The politics of collaborative expertise*. London: Pearson. Accessed at www.pearson.com/content/dam/corporate/global /pearson-dot-com/files/hattie/150526_ ExpertiseWEB_V1.pdf on December 17, 2024.

Hattie, J. (2023). *Visible learning: the sequel: A synthesis of over 2,100 meta-analyses relating to achievement*. New York: Routledge.

Horn, M. B. (2021). *Begin with the end: What's the purpose of schooling?* Accessed at www.forbes.com/sites /michaelhorn/2021/04/15/begin-with-the-end-whats-the-purpose-of-schooling on June 18, 2024.

Junger, S. (2016). *Tribe. On homecoming and belonging*. New York: Twelve.

Kramer, S. (2015). *How to leverage PLCs for school improvement*. Bloomington, IN: Solution Tree Press.

Kramer, S. V., & Schuhl, S. (2017). *School improvement for all: A how-to guide for doing the right work*. Bloomington, IN: Solution Tree Press.

Leane, B. (2018). A vision that changed a school. *Principal Leadership, 18,* 54–57.

Leane, B., & Yost, J. (2022). *Singletons in a PLC at Work: Navigating on-ramps to meaningful collaboration*. Bloomington, IN: Solution Tree Press.

Lencioni, P. (2007). *The three signs of a miserable job: A fable for managers (and their employees)*. San Francisco: Jossey-Bass.

Lencioni, P. (2012). *The advantage: Why organizational health trumps everything else in business*. San Francisco: Jossey-Bass.

Lipton, L., & Wellman, B. (2001). *Mentoring matters: A practical guide to learning focused relationships*. Sherman, CT: MiraVia.

Many, T., & Horrell, T. (2014). Prioritizing the standards using R. E. A. L. criteria. *TEPSA, 71*(1). Accessed at https://absenterprisedotcom.files.wordpress.com/2016/06/real-standards.pdf on March 5, 2024.

Marzano, R. J. (2003). *What works in schools: Translating research into action*. Arlington, VA: ASCD.

Marzano, R. J. (2019). *The handbook for the new art and science of teaching*. Bloomington, IN: Solution Tree Press.

Marzano, R. J., Pickering, D. J, & Pollock, J. E. (2001). *Classroom instruction the works: Research-based strategies for increasing student achievement*. Arlington, VA: ASCD.

Marzano, R. J., Waters, T., & McNulty, B. A. (2005). *School leadership that works: From research to results*. Arlington, VA: ASCD.

Mattos, M., Buffum, A., Malone, J., Cruz, L. F., Dimich, N., & Schuhl, S. (2018). *Taking action: A handbook for RTI at Work* (2nd ed.). Bloomington, IN: Solution Tree Press.

Mattos, M., DuFour, R., DuFour, R., Eaker, R., & Many, T. W. (2016). *Concise answers to frequently asked questions about Professional Learning Communities at Work*. Bloomington, IN: Solution Tree Press.

McChesney, C., Covey, S., & Huling, J. (2012). *The 4 disciplines of execution*. New York: Free Press.

Muhammad, A., & Cruz, L. F. (2019). *Time for change: Four essential skills for transformational school and district leaders*. Bloomington, IN: Solution Tree Press.

Muhammad, A., & Hollie, S. (2012). *The will to lead, the skill to teach: Transforming schools at every level*. Bloomington, IN: Solution Tree Press.

Pink, D. (2009). *Drive: The surprising truth about what motivates us*. New York: Riverhead Books.

Read On Arizona. (2024). *Case studies: Agua Caliente Elementary and Tanque Verde Elementary*. Accessed at https://readonarizona.org/case-studies/TVUSD on April 1, 2024.

Reeves, D. (2000). *Accountability in action. A blueprint for learning organizations*. Denver, CO: Advanced Learning Press.

Reeves, D., & Eaker, R. (2019). The leadership choice: PLCs at Work or PLC Lite? *All Things PLC Magazine*. Bloomington, IN: Solution Tree Press.

Roberts, M. (2020). *Shifting from me to we: How to jump-start collaboration in a PLC at work*. Bloomington, IN: Solution Tree Press.

Schmoker, M. (2006). *Results now: How we can achieve unprecedented improvements in teaching and learning*. Arlington, VA: ASCD.

Silsbee, L. (2023). *The four stages of team development*. Accessed at www.forbes.com/sites/forbescoachescouncil/2023/06/29/the-four-stages-of-team-development/?sh=380ca0e03b2c on March 19, 2024.

Solution Tree. (2024a). *Evidence of excellence: Greater Hartford Academy of the Arts Middle School*. Accessed at www.solutiontree.com/plc-at-work/evidence-of-excellence/greater-hartford-academy on April 1, 2024.

Solution Tree. (2024b). *Evidence of excellence: Minnieville Elementary School*. Accessed at www.solutiontree.com/plc-at-work/evidence-of-excellence/minnieville on April 1, 2024.

Solution Tree. (2024c). *Evidence of excellence: Model PLC at Work and Blue Ribbon Schools*. Accessed at www.solutiontree.com/plc-at-work/evidence-of-excellence/model-plc-and-blue-ribbon-schools on April 1, 2024.

Spiller, J., & Power, K. (2019). *Leading with intention: Eight areas for reflection and planning in your PLC at work*. Bloomington, IN: Solution Tree Press.

Tuckman, B. W. (1965). Developmental sequence in small groups. *Psychological Bulletin, 63*(6), 384–399.

Wiggins, G., & McTighe, J. (2008). Put understanding first. *Educational Leadership, 65*(8). Accessed at www.ascd.org/el/articles/put-understanding-first on June 18, 2024.

Williams, K. C., & Hierck, T. (2015). *Starting a movement. Building culture from the inside out in Professional Learning Communities*. Bloomington, IN: Solution Tree Press.

Williams, K. C. (2022). *Ruthless equity: Disrupt the status quo and ensure learning for all students*. Wish In One Hand Press.

Index

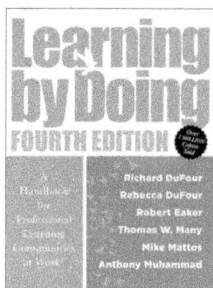

Learning by Doing, Fourth Edition
Richard DuFour, Rebecca DuFour, Robert Eaker, Thomas W. Many, Mike Mattos, and Anthony Muhammad

Twenty-five years on, the PLC at Work® process continues to produce results across the United States and worldwide. In this fourth edition of the bestseller *Learning by Doing*, the authors use updated research and time-tested knowledge to address current education challenges, from learning gaps exacerbated by the COVID-19 pandemic to the need to drive a highly effective multitiered system of supports.
BKG169

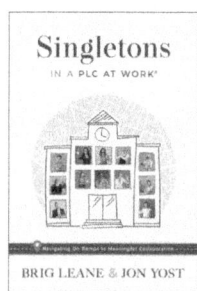

Singletons in a PLC at Work®
Brig Leane and Jon Yost

In a professional learning community, isolation is the enemy of improvement. But what does collaboration look like for teachers who can't easily identify with a team? This book will help singleton teachers first develop clarity on learning essentials, then find creative entry points to form collaborative teams. Drawing from their own experiences, the authors offer practical solutions for eliminating the practice of isolation for all educators.
BKG039

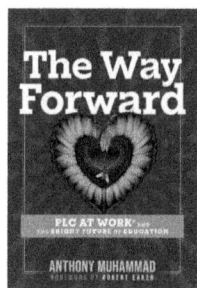

The Way Forward
Anthony Muhammad

Teachers today have a window of opportunity to shape education in a way that will impact the profession for generations. In this compelling and comprehensive book, educator and best-selling author Anthony Muhammad explores the educational hurdles of the past in the context of present-day concerns and envisions an education system where all schools energetically embrace the PLC at Work® process.
BKG159

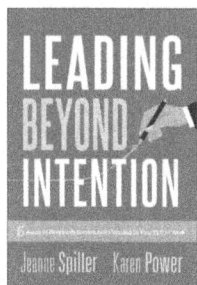

Leading Beyond Intention
Jeanne Spiller and Karen Power

This solutions-focused guide dives deep into personal leadership skills, encourages readers to reflect and grow, and offers practical strategies for weaving the thread of intentionality throughout your daily leadership practice. From building capacity among your staff to finding courage within yourself, you will discover meaningful content that not only provides food for thought but also inspires action.
BKF971

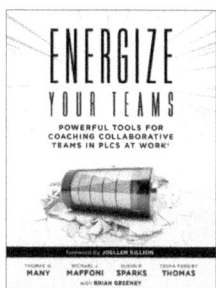

Energize Your Teams
Thomas W. Many, Michael J. Maffoni, Susan K. Sparks, and Tesha Ferriby Thomas

Help your teams get better faster. Written for busy school leaders, instructional coaches, and teacher leaders, this ultimate "grab and grow" guide details how to bridge the gap between learning and doing at every stage of the PLC journey. Rely on the book's ample professional development activities to empower teams to enhance their skills, grow together, and collectively focus on what's working *and* what's next.
BKG009

Solution Tree | Press   *a division of* Solution Tree

Visit SolutionTree.com or call 800.733.6786 to order.

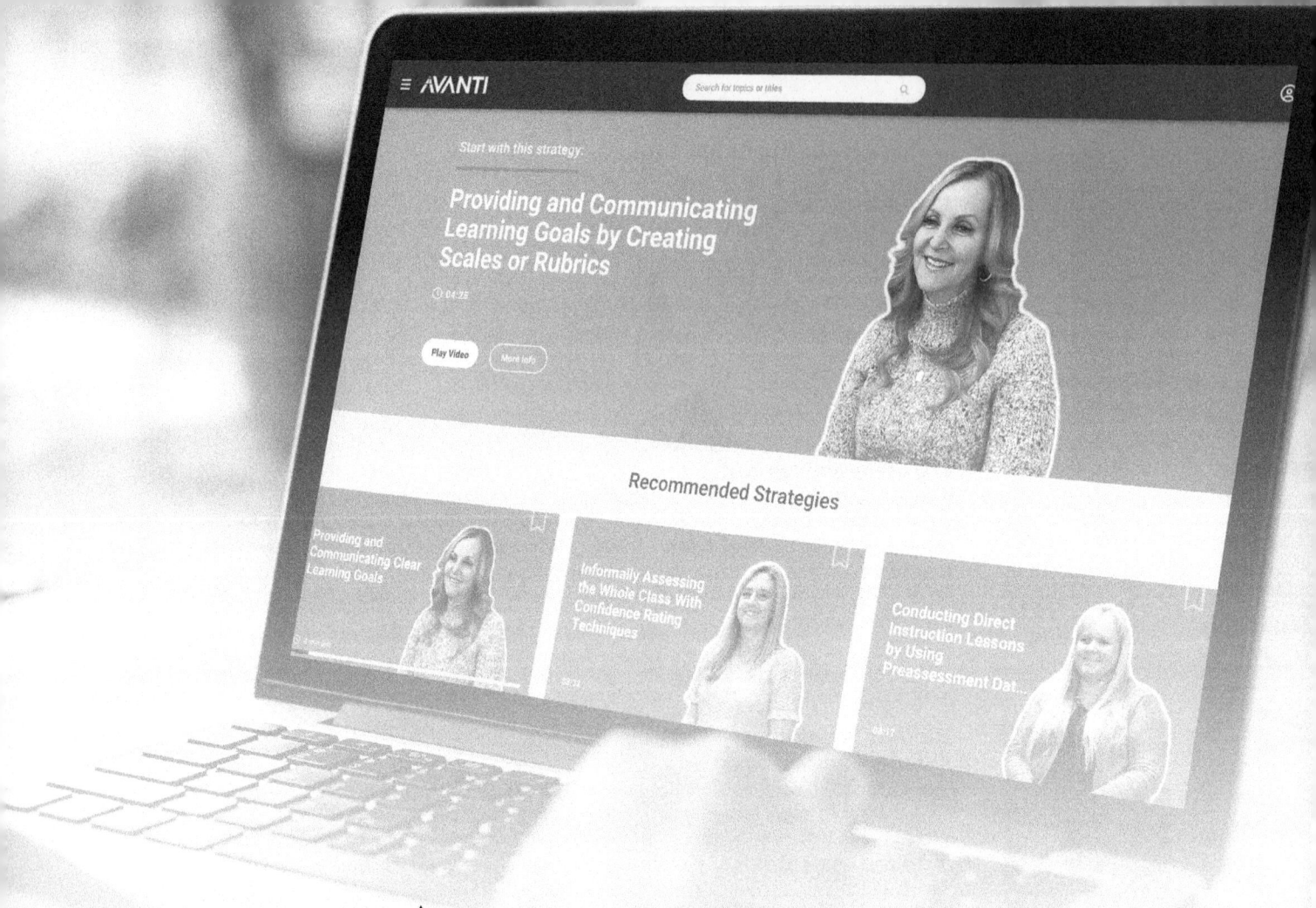